This book is part of the Allyn and Bacon Series in Creative Teaching.

The books in this series are:

I

*Setting Conditions for Creative Teaching
in the Elementary School*
James A. Smith

II

*Creative Teaching of the Language Arts
in the Elementary School*
James A. Smith

III

*Creative Teaching of Reading and Literature
in the Elementary School*
James A. Smith

IV

*Creative Teaching of the Creative Arts
in the Elementary School*
James A. Smith

V

*Creative Teaching of the Social Studies
in the Elementary School*
James A. Smith

VI

*Creative Teaching of Mathematics
in the Elementary School*
Alvin M. Westcott and James A. Smith

VII

*Creative Teaching of Science
in the Elementary School*
Albert Piltz and Robert Sund

Children use their own bodies to explore movement, and through movement communicate feelings and ideas.

Creative Teaching of the Creative Arts

in the Elementary School

James A. Smith
State University of New York at Oswego

foreword by E. Paul Torrance
University of Georgia

ALLYN AND BACON, INC., BOSTON

Library of Congress Catalog Card Number 67-15070

PRINTED IN THE UNITED STATES OF AMERICA

first printing: March, 1967
second printing: April, 1968

to Patricia

Foreword

Many exciting, potentially powerful, and valid educational ideas have gone unused or have been forgotten altogether because no one has translated them into practical methods, instructional materials, textbooks, and the like. The idea of creative teaching has been among them. Creativity has been a persistent and recurrent issue throughout the history of education. Actually, the idea of creative ways of teaching has never had a very good chance to prove its worth. Teachers and educational leaders have continually struggled to understand the nature of creative functioning, the conditions that facilitate and inhibit creative growth, and the means of rewarding creative achievement. Bit by bit, advances have been made, and in recent years efforts to add to this kind of knowledge through research and experimentation have been accelerated. We need to know a great deal more than we do, but in my opinion we have made enough advances to make possible a more creative kind of education than has been known up to now. This is why imaginative, informed, and hard-working translators and creative synthesizers like Professor James A. Smith and his associates, who have created this series of books on setting the conditions for creative teaching and learning, are such a welcome asset to the educational enterprise.

The task of retooling—inventing and testing methods, creating tests and instructional materials, devising evaluation procedures and creating textbooks and methods of teacher education—for any new educational idea is enormous. It takes tremendous energy, creativity, courage, commitment, and willingness to risk on the part of many people. The inauguration of this series of books on creative teaching is a major venture for Professor Smith, his associates, and Allyn and Bacon. In the past, the adoption of new and improved educational ideas has been retarded by two powerful forces—teacher education institutions and textbook publishers. The case of Braille writing for the blind is an excellent example. Even after Louis Braille had perfected the method of writing that bears his name and had tested it successfully for five years, it was not adopted by schools for the blind. Opposition came from the training institutions because teachers would have to master this new way of writing and from textbook publishers because they would lose their investments in the enormous embossed books then used by the blind. It was not until many years after Braille's death that his method of writing for the blind was adopted.

Innovations in education are usually hailed as "fads" that will soon be forgotten. This is a common expression of resistance to change. Rarely, however, are valid and worthwhile innovations really forgotten, if they are translated into tested methods and materials. Braille had created an alphabet, a way of writing, that had been taught successfully to blind children. The idea of Braille writing could be rejected but it could not be forgotten. Similar statements might be made about the educational innovations of people like Socrates, Froebel, Montessori, and others. They created and tested methods and materials that have been rejected for a time, but the world has not been able to forget them. Many people have said that the idea of a more creative education is a fad that will pass and soon be forgotten. It *is* possible that creative ways of teaching may be rejected, but they will not be forgotten. Professor Smith and his co-authors in this seven-volume series have in a variety of ways expressed the definition, the spirit, and the truths of creative teaching in a way that will be difficult to forget.

The format of each book of this seven-volume series illustrates concretely many of the most important principles of creative teaching. Through the format and structure of these books, the author and publisher recognize the reader as self-acting and stimulus-seeking. The reader is provided both the guidance and the freedom necessary for creative growth. These books are a rich source of ideas, but this is not their greatest value. The reader who uses them for rapid reading or for occasional reference will miss an important opportunity for personal growth and professional development in creative directions. The "great ideas" quoted at the beginning of chapters are provocative. The suggested activities preceding most chapters provide worthwhile explorations in creativity. The content of the chapters provides a wealth of information that translates research findings into classroom methods and instructional materials. The exercises and questions at the end of each chapter will help the reader to make a creative synthesis of these experiences.

The authors offer themselves as models of creative teaching.

They bring to their task the fresh aroma of first-hand experiences in creative teaching in the college and university classroom and in elementary schools. They also offer the reader a variety of other models of creative teaching, making him feel almost as though "he were there." Participation in the experiences of the authors and the teachers they have observed, however, is not enough. The authors have added to this the kind of guidance that helps the reader identify, understand, and generalize the important principles at work in these experiences. This should increase the chances that the reader will develop useful skills and be able to transform his own classroom behavior.

Each of the seven books has its own unique contribution, along with a consistent philosophy. Book I is a creative synthesis of Professor Smith's rich experience in teaching children and teachers of children, a vast amount of research concerning creativity and classroom learning, and his theories of education. It is far more than this, however. The author has gone beyond all of these and, building onto the contributions of others, added his own innovations. He has distilled a great deal of the essence of the creativity of children. Book II, *Creative Teaching of the Language Arts in the Elementary School,* is a comprehensive, well-organized, and rich source of ideas. Book III, *Creative Teaching of Reading and Literature in the Elementary School,* is perhaps my own favorite. It is interesting and exciting and assumes a positive and consistent position on important issues in teaching reading. It will be difficult for the reader to resist becoming a creative reader. The way in which the author heightens expectations and challenges the reader to do things with what he reads is quite compelling. The books on social studies, science, the arts, and mathematics have their own unique features and should be valuable in courses on teaching methods in these areas and to teachers in service who want to become more skilled in setting the conditions for creative learning.

It is my own hope that your creative use of this series of books will help you realize more fully your own dream of helping your pupils live more creatively. This is the challenge of our day. In the past, we have been able to survive with static goals and concepts. This is no longer true. Things are changing so rapidly that our civilization can no longer survive if we insist on thinking and living in static terms and returning to the "old ways."

E. PAUL TORRANCE
University of Georgia

Preface

I recently asked a class of college juniors how much they remembered about their art and music classes when they were in the elementary school. I then asked them if they would list for me those objectives which they felt the art and music teachers had in mind when they taught these classes. The results were interesting.

Most of the students remembered having an art and music teacher. Some remembered art and music activities carried on by the regular classroom teacher when the special teacher was not in the room, but most could remember no such experience. About half of them remembered art and music pleasantly: they looked forward to it and enjoyed the lessons but the other half were indifferent or expressed downright distaste for art and music periods.

Without an exception they all listed the following as objectives of the art and music programs: (1) to develop an appreciation for the fine arts and (2) to teach elementary school children to draw. Ninety percent of the group agreed on the following additional objectives: (1) to develop self-expression in children; (2) to provide an outlet for creative expression and (3) to encourage aesthetic living. A smattering of other objectives appeared but the five above were the ones they recognized as most important.

I then asked the students to take their list of five objectives with them and observe life around them for a week and to determine whether or not they felt these objectives had been accomplished.

The results were discouraging. Most of them felt that a majority of people today had little appreciation of art or music. They pointed out the resistance they experienced among their peers and their parents to new art forms such as modern art and to new music forms such as rock and roll. They recounted how, on the first day of class, they had panicked when I asked them to draw something for me. They also admitted their reluctance to express themselves before their peers or their professors with any kind of individuality in art, music, poetry, literature or dramatics except in a few classes where they were forced to do so because their grades relied on it. They pointed out the vulgarity of our cities, the lack of aesthetic planning for beauty as well as functionalism, the lack of respect shown for beautiful things. One girl mentioned that some student in the class that day had hung her raincoat over a beautiful shadow box arrangement of flowers which the instructor had placed at the front of the room.

We then set to work trying to arrive at a mean which would indicate the average number of hours each had spent in an art and music class between kindergarten and Grade 6. They arrived at a mean of nine thousand hours for art and music each! We then estimated the amount of money it had cost to hire art and music teachers (in terms of present-day salaries) and the amount of money spent on supplies, equipment and instruments for all of those six years. The end estimate was about $75,000.

All that money and all that time to meet five objectives which obviously had not been met! When I posed the question, "Why?" I began to get some very creative and critical thinking.

But—why? In this particular class I had the cream of the crop of our young people: all from backgrounds where there was *some* exposure to the finer things of life; all from high or above-average socio-economic conditions; all with above average intelligence. So, indeed, why? Why in the past two decades have we failed to develop in the majority of human beings in this great democratic society at least the minimum essentials of aesthetic living and basic principles of creativity to which *all* were exposed as children (compulsory education laws made this inevitable)?

The answer can only lie in the fact that much of the teaching was voided by the *way* in which it was taught. At first glance the title of this book, *Setting Conditions for the Creative Teaching of the Creative Arts,* may appear to be a contradiction. But, in light of the above experience, it is not. Although the teaching of Creative Arts in our elementary schools has done more than any other area of the curriculum to develop creativity, the fact still remains that it has not developed the creativity in *all* children as it was intended to do. Judging from the attitudes of many young adults, both in college and out, it has often resulted in the exact opposite; most of them are *afraid* to be creative and to seek other, less positive, less rewarding outlets for their creative emotions.

It is only in the last decade that we have come to understand what creativity is and how it can be developed. We are now able to comprehend why certain art programs and music programs killed off the creative power in children, and voided the bookish objectives listed above by my college juniors. The objectives can still stand— they are sound and proper; but the method of accomplishing them must go, for they have shown themselves to be unsound and unproductive for the majority of children.

Creativity has become a precious commodity in the Space Age. It is precious because it is necessary to our survival. We need creative people to solve the problems of modern living. History will not help us too much for the problems have never before existed; their solution lies in the *creative* minds of men! We also need creative people in order to fulfill our political destiny. In a democratic society individuals count—but they are able to stand up and be counted only if they are *individuals!*

Creativity cannot be developed solely in one or two art lessons a week, or in one or two music lessons a week. It is a quality at which we must work in order to develop it to its full potential in every human being. It can be developed through exploiting every area of the curriculum *if we can develop it in the teachers of our children* so they, in turn, can become creative teachers.

That's what this series of books is about: showing teachers how creativity can be developed in the children of our schools through the exploitation of all areas of the curriculum. This volume concentrates on the Creative Arts. It is a companion volume to Book I: *Setting Conditions for Creative Teaching in the Elementary School.* Other volumes in the set explore the manner by which creativity can be developed in the teaching of the Language Arts (Book II), in the teaching of Reading and Literature (Book III), in the teaching of the Social Studies (Book IV), in the teaching of Mathematics (Book VI) and in the teaching of Science (Book VII).

Because an understanding of Book I is necessary in order to comprehend the current volume, Chapter I offers a summary of the basic principles of creative teaching and an understanding of creative development as they are proposed in the first volume of the set. The remainder of the volume concentrates on the development of the creative powers of children and proposes ways by which teachers may become "bridging engineers" in putting the research on creativity into common schoolroom practice.

None of the books in the series is intended to be a cookbook. Here, in essence, is one reason why teaching for creativity in the past has failed. Too often children have been exploited as middle-men for the art, music and classroom teacher and have served the major function of bringing into reality a preconceived product born in the mind of these teachers and subject to unjust evaluation when it did not result in a form congruent with the preconception.

These books are written with two groups of people in mind: the college student in teacher education and the teacher in service.

The author wishes to express his appreciation to all the people to whom he is indebted for materials in this book. Among them are the many children who granted him permission to use their materials, his creative teacher-colleagues who tried many of the ideas in this book on their children, his own college students and especially his student teachers who dared to be creative and allowed him to watch them at work, and to the many teachers and student teachers who "loaned" him their classrooms and their children so he could try many of his own ideas.

Special acknowledgment must be made to the following people: Dr. Michael Andrews of Syracuse University for his constant inspiration; Mrs. Sally Pomeroy, music teacher in the Liverpool School System who provided access to her materials and many happy hours of observation.

Lastly, to my own daughter, Patricia, who has demonstrated to me how fanning the creative spark and supplying the flame with the fuel of motivation and encouragement can develop creative thinking and creative results, and what is more important, a beautiful soul. To her he dedicates this book.

JAMES A. SMITH
Oswego, N.Y.

Contents

Part One: The Nature of the Creative Arts | 1

I The Nature of Creative Teaching | 3

Introduction | 3
What is Creativity? | 4
Basic Principles of Creative Teaching | 6
Summary | 12

II The Nature of Teaching in the Creative Arts: Art | 17

Introduction | 17
The Nature of Art | 18
The Role of the Specialist | 39
Experience and Application | 43
Summary | 44

III The Nature of Teaching in the Creative Arts:
Music, Dance and Dramatics | 49

The Nature of Music | 49
The Nature of Rhythms and Dance | 53
The Nature of Creative Dramatics | 55
Summary | 60

Part Two: The Nurture of Creativity Through the Creative Arts | 65

IV Creative Teaching Through Art | 67

Introduction | 67
Summary | 90

V Creative Teaching Through Music | 95

Introduction | 95
Suggestions for Setting Conditions
for Primary Music Activities | 105
Suggestions for Developing Creativity
Through Intermediate Grade Activities | 113
Summary | 124

VI   **Creative Teaching Through Rhythms and Dance**   **129**

 Introduction   *129*
 Conditions Necessary for Creative Development
  Through the Dance   *130*
 The Teacher's Role   *136*
 Developing Creativity Through the Use of Rhythms
  and Dance in the Primary Grades   *138*
 Developing Creativity Through Use of the Dance
  in the Intermediate Grades   *144*
 Summary   *146*

VII   **Creative Teaching Through Dramatization**   **150**

 Introduction   *150*
 Situations Which Set Conditions for Dramatic Play
  in the Primary Grades   *155*
 Situations Which Set Conditions for Creative
  Development Through Dramatic Play in the
  Intermediate Grades   *159*
 Situations Which Set Conditions for the Development of
  Creativity Through Dramatics in the Intermediate
  Grades   *161*
 Summary   *170*

VIII   **Conclusion: The Creative Teacher**   **174**

 Introduction   **174**

Index   **183**

Part One

The Nature of the Creative Arts

I
The Nature of Creative Teaching

Good teachers are guided by the deep conviction that the potentiality for creative experience belongs to all children. They know that, although the abilities among individual children vary widely, understanding, encouragement, and help lead children to develop the abilities they have.[1]

MANUEL BARKAN

TO THE READER

The material in this chapter is a summary of Book I, Setting Conditions for Creative Teaching in the Elementary School. *I advise you to read that volume as a companion to this book. This summary chapter will help you pull from Book I all of those principles especially related to the teaching of the Creative Arts.*

Introduction

Creativity cannot be taught. We can only set conditions for it to happen. Because it is a quality deeply imbedded in the human personality, it can be developed by re-enforcement when it does appear, but the main function of the creative teacher is to maintain certain physical, psychological, socio-emotional and intellectual conditions within her classroom so that creativity will be free to rise to the surface where she can reach and develop it. The *conditions* set for developing creativity, then, become very important in the regular classroom. Under proper conditions it may become a quality possessed by every child.

Research in the past decade in the area of creativity has been extensive. This research has helped us to understand creativity, what it is, the characteristics of the creative person and some of the ways it can be developed.

[1] Manuel Barkan, *Through Art to Creativity* (Boston: Allyn and Bacon, Inc., 1960), p. 1.

What Is Creativity?

Creativity, in this volume, is defined as the ability to tap past experiences and come up with something new. This product need not be new to the world but it must be new to the individual, though the most creative acts are those which result in something new to the world.

Basic Principles of Creativity

Research in the area of creativity has guided this author in compiling a set of principles which were fully developed in Book I of this series.[2] A review of this list follows, forming a foundation for this volume.

1. *All children are born creative.* Creativity is not a special talent doled out to a chosen few. It is present in every individual, though it varies in degree. Its development depends largely on both environment and intelligence.

2. *There is a relationship between creativity and intelligence.* Highly creative people are always highly intelligent people but highly intelligent people are not always creative. Although creativity is a form of giftedness inherent to some degree in each individual, intelligence determines the quality of the creative product. Even slow learning children are creative, however.

3. *Creativity is a form of giftedness which is not measured by current intelligence tests.* J. P. Guilford[3] explains that our creative powers are developed through the exercise of our divergent thinking abilities and that this component of the intellect has been grossly neglected in our elementary schools. Almost all learning has been conceived as developing the convergent thinking processes. Convergent thinking processes are those where the child comes up with one answer—a correct answer, while in divergent thinking processes many answers are possible, and uniqueness of answer may be the important factor in solving a problem. All intelligence tests up to this

  [2] James A. Smith, *Setting Conditions for Creative Teaching in the Elementary School* (Boston: Allyn and Bacon, Inc., 1966).

  [3] J. P. Guilford, "Three Faces of Intellect," *American Psychologist,* XIV, 1959, pp. 469–479.

time measure only convergent thinking processes and therefore do not measure creativity.

4. *All areas of the curriculum may be used to develop creativity.* The development of creativity is not limited to a program in the creative arts. Creativity, as this series of books shows, can be developed through all areas of the curriculum; it is not something to be added to the heavy schedules of teachers, or something that should be taught at a given period once or twice a week, but a quality, a characteristic and a *way* of learning. Some research has shown that creative learning excels more traditional methods both in quantity and quality, and that creative learning calls for creative teaching.

5. *Creativity is a process and a product.* Although research is not conclusive in this area, most researchers will accept the following steps as those which human beings go through in the creative process. Mary Lee Marksberry has identified these steps in her recent book, *Foundation of Creativity,*[4] as being part of the creative act:

a. *Period of preparation:* The creator becomes involved with and identifies with the problem at hand.
b. *Period of incubation:* The creator lives with and is even tormented by the problem.
c. *Period of insight:* All parts of the problem seem to become clear.
d. *Period of illumination or inspiration:* Ideas or answers seem to come; this may also be classified as a moment of discovery.
e. *Period of verification, elaboration, perfection and evaluation:* The product is tested for its worth; tension is relieved.

6. *All creative processes cannot be developed at one time or in one lesson.* The total personality of the creative person is made up of many characteristics, skills and qualities, each of which may be developed when teaching is directed toward it. Just as all skills in reading cannot be developed in one lesson, each of the components of creativity may be a target for instruction, thus contributing to the development of those qualities, skills and characteristics which make the creative individual. Therefore the development of creativity, affected by the environment into which it is placed, requires a long period of time.

7. *Creativity cannot be taught.* Although some of the component parts of the creative character (such as visual acuity, evalua-

---

[4] Mary Lee Marksberry, *Foundation of Creativity* (New York: Harper & Row, Publishers, Inc., 1963).

tion skills, and comprehension skills) can be taught, total creativity, as such, is not taught. We can only set conditions for it and insure its reappearance through re-enforcement. Chapter II deals with those conditions necessary to develop creativity through the teaching of the creative arts.

8. *More knowledge, more skills and more facts are required of each individual in order for him to be creative than ever before.* The more the individual has to work with, the higher his production will be.

9. *Theories of creative development lead us to believe that the unconscious plays a role in creative development.* Children must be free to tap all of life's experiences in order to become truly creative. Unnecessary rules and actions may force many experiences into the subconscious where they are not available to the child. He is afraid of losing social status if he taps this resource for the purpose of creating.

If a child has difficulty in drawing, for instance, it means he has not had or does not remember having a highly personal reaction with the object he is trying to draw and its environment. It is better to help him recall or enter again into his past experience with the object, or to give him a new experience with the object, than it is to give him stereotyped patterns to copy.

10. *Excessive conformity and rigidity are true enemies of creativity.* Conformity is necessary to maintain a society, but conformity is the one greatest known killers of creative development.

11. *Children go through definite steps in the creative process.* These steps were outlined above in No. 5.

12. *Creative teaching and creative learning can be more effective than other types of teaching and learning.* See No. 4, above.

13. *Children who have lost much of their creativity may be helped to regain it by special methods of teaching.* This, of course, means the employment of *methods* of creative teaching in the classroom. These methods are derived from a set of basic principles culled from research on creativity.

Basic Principles of Creative Teaching

Following is a condensed explanation of the basic principles of creative teaching as they were developed in *Setting Conditions for Creative Teaching in the Elementary School.*[5]

[5] James A. Smith, *Setting Conditions for Creative Teaching in the Elementary School* (Boston: Allyn and Bacon, Inc., 1966).

1. *From creative teaching something new, different or unique results.* In the creative teaching of the creative arts every piece of sculpture, every painting, every poem or song is different from all others. Because children tap their own experiences, and because these experiences are each different in perception and form, every interpretation is unique. No two people can *create* the same thing.

2. *In creative teaching, divergent thinking processes are stressed.* Divergent thinking processes do not produce an absolute or correct answer. In divergent thinking, knowledges, facts, concepts, understandings and skills gained through convergent thinking are put to new uses resulting in new answers rather than in one correct answer. Divergent thinking processes develop such qualities as flexibility, fluency, spontaneity and originality, and are the bases of creative thinking. It has been pointed out above that creativity is a kind of giftedness and the current I.Q. tests do not measure divergent thinking processes and therefore do not identify creativity gifted children, but only intellectually gifted ones.

In teaching the creative arts the teacher is provided with innumerable opportunities to develop the divergent functions of the intellect. Learning how to mix a powder paint is an example of a memorization of facts and illustrates convergent thinking processes. The actual free form painting which follows is an example of the divergent thinking process. All paintings are unique; all are acceptable.

3. *In creative teaching, motivational tensions are a prerequisite to the creative process: the process serves as a tension-relieving agent.* Motivation is essential to all learning but this is particularly true in creative development. The "passion for learning" suggested above must plague the creator—the drive to use the right word in the right place, the right color in the right place, the right note in the right place. Although many children will paint and compose spontaneously, the introduction to the lesson which sets the mood and fires the children's imagination must be planned with great care.

4. *In creative teaching, open-ended situations are utilized.* Open-endedness in teaching means presenting children with situations where they put their knowledges, understandings and skills to work. The one great difference between lessons which develop convergent thinking processes and those which develop divergent thinking processes is that in the former the lesson ends when knowledge is gained while in the latter, a situation is provided in which newly acquired knowledge is put to work to solve a problem. The acquisition of knowledge *begins* the divergent thought process.

5. *In creative teaching, there comes a time when the teacher withdraws and the children face the unknown themselves.* At this moment the teacher and the children change roles. The teacher, in building high motivational tensions, is the planner, the guide and the producer. At one point in the lesson she withdraws from this role and the children, spurred on by the tensions she has created, become the planners, the guides and the producers. Each leads himself to the fulfillment of the creative act. It is an essential part of the creative act that each individual solve the problem in his own way, arriving at his own unique solution or product.

6. *In creative teaching, the outcomes are unpredictable.* Another unique quality of the creative teaching process is that the teacher cannot know exactly what the product will be. In teaching an arithmetic lesson, the process may be very creative, but the teacher knows at the onset of the lesson that the children (with the possible exception of a few slow ones) will learn the correct answers and how to obtain them by the end of the lesson; in teaching for creative production, the teacher cannot know what the products will be. She must possess the power to motivate children to produce, and faith that their creative products will be worthy of the time spent.

7. *In creative teaching, conditions must be set which make possible preconscious thinking.* Children are encouraged constantly to draw from their experiences. Ideas are not considered silly or impossible, but each is evaluated. Conformity to preconceived rules is omitted. If a child decides he would like to try to finger paint with his knuckles or the palm of his hand, he is encouraged to do so even if a previous teacher has told him to use only his fingers. The rigid, conforming rules under which children often labor for status or approval are relaxed. A further development of the basic psychological conditions necessary for creative development follows. (A detailed account of such situations is developed in Book I, Chapter III.)[6]

8. *Creative teaching means that students are encouraged to generate and develop their own ideas.* Research in identifying the creative personality indicates that creative children are often treated along punitive lines by their teachers and are considered to have silly and senseless ideas. Yet, many of the world's greatest inventions and discoveries have come from such silly ideas. Unusual and even silly ideas are the threshold of creative discovery and must be encouraged if creativity is to be developed.

[6] *Ibid.,* pp. 36–40.

9. *In creative teaching, differences, uniqueness, individuality, originality are stressed and rewarded.* This provides the re-enforcement which causes creativity to appear again and again so we can work with it.

10. *In creative teaching, the process is as important as the product.* The process of creative production as defined above by Marksberry occurs more frequently among children when it is deliberately repeated so practice is afforded in creative thinking. In some instances creativity is fostered more readily by the process than the product, as would be the case in the creative teaching of arithmetic (see Book VI of this series, *Creative Teaching of Mathematics in the Elementary School*).[7]

11. *In creative teaching, certain conditions must be set to permit creativity to appear.* The unique conditions necessary to develop creative production in the creative arts will be developed in the next chapter. However, there are some general conditions necessary to all creative production. Most obvious among these are certain *physical conditions*. The classroom must be a learning laboratory with material readily available and arranged in such a manner that the task at hand can be accomplished.

Certain *psychological* conditions are also necessary. Good rapport must exist between teacher and children and among the children themselves; they must be comfortable with and accept each other. An "air of expectancy" must pervade; children must feel that they are expected to create. The atmosphere must be permissive to the degree that children feel comfortable experimenting, manipulating and exploring. They must feel free to make mistakes. A great deal of uncertainty is present in the creative act when children face the unknown and they will be more secure if their creative behavior is rooted in psychological securities such as those mentioned above.

Teaching must be success-oriented rather than failure-oriented. As mentioned above, failure may be used as a motivating force of creative production. There is a difference between failure experiences and failure. Failure experiences help children understand the true conditions of life and build character, but repeated failure can only result in psychological damage to personalities and a lowering of self-esteem.

Certain *intellectual* conditions must also prevail if creative development is to take place. Children must be motivated to think;

---

[7] Alvin M. Westcott and James A. Smith, *Creative Teaching of Mathematics in the Elementary School* (Boston: Allyn and Bacon, Inc., 1967).

their imagination must be teased by problems posed in such a way that they are all thinking most of the time. A great many facts and skills must be available to each child, some of which will be taught by convergent thinking processes but put to divergent uses. The more knowledge, skills, and facts a child has the more there is available to his use when he taps his experiences in order to create.

Sound *social* and *emotional* conditions must prevail in a comfortable relationship among the children. Children who are emotionally upset may often find outlets for their pent-up emotions in creative products if the proper social climate, one of acceptance and understanding, exists. Under such circumstances, creative energy may be dispelled in creative, constructive acts rather than uncreative, destructive acts.

12. *Creative teaching is success rather than failure oriented.* Disapproval, sarcasm, and other forms of verbal punishment may often be interpreted by the child who experiences them as failure. Negative criticism is dangerous unless a creative relationship has been established between the teacher and the student. Once this rapport is established, criticism and disapproval, used with a constructive goal rather than as punishment, may be useful.

Even at the onset of the creative act, excessive evaluation may be construed by children as disapproval and may check their flow of creative ideas. The work of many researchers (see 18 below) concludes that evaluation and criticism of ideas be postponed until all ideas are out. This is often called "the principle of deferred judgment."

The creative child must be willing to make mistakes but he needs to develop skills for finding out when he makes a mistake and how to correct it. A set of criteria may be worked out with the child for evaluating ideas so the child understands that criticism, disapproval or rejection of his ideas are made because they are not the best, and not because they are unworthy of consideration. The ability of the teacher to turn failures into successes keeps her teaching success-oriented because failures are utilized as a base for a more appropriate solution to the problem.

13. *In creative teaching, provision is made to learn many knowledges and skills but provision is also made to apply these knowledges and skills to new problem-solving situations.* Learning to read music is a skill which can be learned by convergent thought processes, but the skill is best retained when children create and record their own music.

14. *In creative teaching, self-initiated learning is encouraged.*

The release of tensions accompanied by the aesthetic satisfactions which come with the creation of a new product or with the working through of a problem make the creative process cyclic. This release and satisfaction becomes a part of the high motivation required for successive creative acts. Children become truly creative when they constantly occupy themselves with self-imposed problems and produce poems, paintings, dances, songs and other creative products without the continual motivation of the teacher.

15. *In creative teaching, skills of constructive criticism and evaluation skills are developed.* Many convergent thought processes are essential to the full development of creative thinking. For example the application of evaluation skill is an aid if it is practiced at the conclusion of the creative act.[8] A set of criteria worked out with the child to measure the effectiveness or the usefulness of his creative products will help him to be constructively critical and to evaluate effectively.

16. *In creative teaching, ideas and objects are manipulated and explored.* Research shows that the more children are allowed to discover, manipulate, explore, experiment with, and resolve their own failures, the more creative they become.

17. *Creative teaching employs democratic processes.* Because creativity is individualism and because a basic principle to democratic ideology is that individuals are important, the development of democratic procedures in the classroom develops creativity in children. No person ever became great or famous by copying that which other individuals have already accomplished. In order to become self-realized as a democratic citizen, each person must remain an individual, helping the total culture to move forward by contributing his own unique ideas. This goal is synonymous with that of creative development, and true democratic living in the classroom calls for the development of the individual powers of each student—all the creative power he can muster. Creative people are needed in our country today more than ever before. There is keen competition throughout the world for the creative minds of men.

18. *In creative teaching, methods are used which are unique to the development of creativity.* Among these special methods are those suggested by Alex Osborn[9] and Sidney Parnes[10] in their courses on

[8] Sidney J. Parnes, *Instructor's Manual for Semester Courses in Creative Problem Solving* (Buffalo: The Creative Foundation, 1963, rev. ed.) pp. 32–66.

[9] Alex F. Osborn, *Applied Imagination* (New York: Charles Scribner's Sons, 1963, third rev. ed.).

[10] Sidney J. Parnes, *Instructor's Manual for Semester Courses in Creative Problem Solving* (Buffalo: The Creative Foundation, 1963, rev. ed.).

Creative Problem-Solving at the University of Buffalo:

    a. *Deferred judgment.* No evaluation of ideas is offered until after all ideas and creative products are reviewed.

    b. *Creative ideation.* Dr. Osborn suggests that to stretch creative thinking we apply the following criteria to creative products: new uses, adaptiveness, modification, magnification, minification, substitution, rearrangement, reversing and combining. Dr. Parnes suggests attribute listing, forced relationships and structure analysis.

Summary

There is a decided difference in the methodology of creative teaching and that of traditional teaching. In the area of the fine arts over any other area, homage has been paid to these differences. But even the fine arts curriculum has not been free from violations and abuses of the creative powers of children. Research in the past decade has provided us with a fuller understanding of creativity and the manner in which it develops. The job of the elementary school has always been to develop those component parts of the intellect which are necessary to life in a democratic society, and today creative powers are needed more than ever before.

The basic principles of creativity and creative teaching as summarized in this chapter provide the framework for our future action. Now that we know a great deal about creativity and how it is developed, we can wed it to our knowledge of the fine arts and avoid blunders such as those made in the past. Because people have been more receptive to innovation and individuality in the fine arts than in other areas of the school curriculum, this area offers the greatest opportunity for the first giant step in revising methodology currently employed by most schools. In the succeeding chapters examples and ideas translate into action the principles discussed in this chapter.

TO THE COLLEGE STUDENT

1. Identify five great teachers from history. Read about them and decide which ones were creative in their approach to teaching. One group of students included in their list such names as Socrates,

Confucius, Jesus, John Dewey, Marie Montessori, Helen Keller and Buddha. Would you include these on your list? Write a description about a great teacher under whom you have studied.

2. Do some research on the Montessori method of teaching and decide on its creative and non-creative aspects.

3. Send for and examine some tests which measure creativity. What aspects of giftedness do these tests explore which the standard intelligence test does not? Ask you college psychologist to give a demonstration of this test with a child.

4. Using the material in this chapter as a reference, construct items which might be used with your college peers to measure their creativity.

5. Discuss ways you could measure the creative teaching abilities of a teacher. Devise some items to fit your plans.

6. Can you think of other forms of giftedness that might not be measured by intelligence tests? List them.

7. List as many ways as you can that dramatics may be used to develop creativity.

8. Do the same for the dance.

9. Check your own creativity by some of the following exercises:

   a. Think of all the ways you can use a moving picture in the classroom.
   b. Think of all the ways that audio-visual aids may be used to develop creativity.
   c. Think of all the ways that textbooks and workbooks can be used to develop creativity.
   d. Can arithmetic be taught creatively? How?

TO THE CLASSROOM TEACHER

1. Can you identify the creative children in your classroom? How? Could you devise a check sheet of items which would help you, using the material in this chapter as a reference?

2. Can you identify the creative teachers in your school? What do you look for in doing so?

3. Think of all the things you are now doing which help in the development of creativity such as building visual acuity and comprehension skills in your reading program, developing evaluation skills in social studies, etc. Make a list of the characteristics which develop creativity as they are described in this chapter indicating which ones you are already working on in your instructional program.

4. Which of the following sets of statements are likely to produce strong motivational tensions in children?

  a. "Listen carefully while I explain each step of the dance. Once you know the pattern we will listen to the music."
    or
    "I have a very exciting dance record here. Listen and show me what it tells you to do."

  b. "Now that we have read the story, let's make a play from it. I will have each of you read some parts. The best ones will be chosen for the play."
    or
    "Now that we have read the story, can you work in groups and tell it in some new and different way?"

  c. "When I nod my head all of you hit your instruments to go to the beat in the music."
    or
    "Now that each of you has chosen an instrument, let's let each person show us what he can do with it."

5. In the above sets of quotations, which ones are apt to produce creative results?

6. Teachers can set conditions for developing creativity simply by the things they say. An example of this is shown in Manuel Barkan's book, *Through Art to Creativity* (Boston: Allyn and Bacon, 1960). Read it and observe carefully how creative teachers employ this skill.

TO THE COLLEGE STUDENT AND
THE CLASSROOM TEACHER

1. Think of all the ways you can develop creativity in the creative arts through the language arts (see Book II of this series, *Creative Teaching of the Language Arts in the Elementary School*),

the teaching of literature (see Book III, *Creative Teaching of Reading and Literature in the Elementary School*) and the social studies (see Book V, *Creative Teaching of the Social Studies in the Elementary School*).

2. Have you often felt your classroom inadequate to carry on the activities you want to? Design the ideal classroom.

3. In light of the discussion in this chapter do you think that creative products in the elementary classroom can be graded with letter or number grades? Discuss this.

4. Place a colored plastic ball before you on the table. Make a list of all the uses to which it could be put. After you have made such a list see if you can stretch it by considering Osborne and Parnes's suggestions for creative ideation:

   a. To what *new uses* could I put it? (Perhaps use it as a Christmas tree ornament, or a party decoration.)
   b. How can I *adapt* it to other purposes? (Tape ribbons to it and suspend it from the ceiling as a decoration.)
   c. Can I *modify* it so it can be used differently? (Fasten it to a tray and garnish it to resemble a pudding for a prop in *The Christmas Carol.*)
   d. Can I *magnify* it? (Add other balls to it to make a cluster of grapes to decorate a large ballroom.)
   e. Can I *minify* it? (Perhaps use it as the base of a puppet head by pasting on hair, eyes and lips and putting it on a stick.)
   f. Can I *combine* it with something else? (How about No. 4 above or how about adding a waste paper basket to it to invent a new version of a basketball game?)
   g. Can I *substitute* something else for it? (You could substitute a balloon, a styrofoam ball or a round bowl.)

5. Try some of the above suggestions on your children when they are trying to make scenery for a play, or props, or costumes.

SELECTED BIBLIOGRAPHY

ANDERSON, HAROLD H. (ed.). *Creativity and Its Cultivation.* New York: Harper & Row, Publishers, Inc., 1959.
ASHTON-WARNER, SYLVIA. *Teacher.* New York: Bantam Books, 1963.

BRYSON, L. "Training for Creativity," *School Arts,* LV (September, 1960), 5–8.

FRYE, NORTHROP. *The Educated Imagination.* Bloomington: Indiana University Press, 1964.

GHISELIN, BREWSTER (ed.). *The Creative Process.* New York: Mentor Books, 1955.

GUILFORD, JOY P. "Factors that Aid and Hinder Creativity," *Teachers College Record,* LXIII (February, 1962), 380–92.

MACKINNON, DONALD W. "What Makes a Person Creative?" *Saturday Review* (February 10, 1962).

MARKSBERRY, MARY L. *Foundation of Creativity.* New York: Harper & Row, Publishers, Inc., 1963.

MEARNS, HUGHES. *Creative Power: The Education of Youth in the Creative Arts,* 2nd rev. ed. New York: Dover Publications, 1959.

MIEL, ALICE (ed.). *Creativity in Teaching.* Belmont: Wadsworth Publishing Co., Inc., 1961.

MURPHY, GARDNER. *Human Potentialities.* New York: Basic Books, Inc., 1958.

OSBORN, ALEX F. *Applied Imagination,* rev. ed. New York: Charles Scribner's Sons, 1963.

RUGG, HAROLD. *Imagination: An Inquiry into the Sources and Conditions that Stimulate Creativity.* New York: Harper & Row, Publishers, Inc., 1963.

SMITH, JAMES A. *Creativity: Its Nature and Nurture.* Syracuse: Syracuse University Press, 1964.

TAYLOR, CALVIN W. *Creativity: Progress and Potential.* New York: McGraw-Hill Book Co., 1964.

———. "Clues to Creative Teaching," *The Instructor* (September 1963—June 1964).

TORRANCE, E. PAUL (ed.) *Creativity.* Minneapolis: University of Minnesota, Center for Continuation Study of the General Extension Division, 1959.

———. *Guiding Creative Talent.* Englewood Cliffs: Prentice-Hall, Inc., 1962.

———. *Rewarding Creative Behavior.* Englewood Cliffs: Prentice-Hall, Inc., 1965.

VON FANGE, E. K. *Professional Creativity.* Englewood Cliffs: Prentice-Hall, Inc., 1959.

WERTHEIMER, M. *Productive Thinking.* New York: Harper & Row, Publishers, Inc., 1959.

WILT, MARION E. *Creativity in the Elementary School.* New York: Appleton-Century-Crofts, Inc., 1959.

ZIRBES, LAURA. *Spurs to Creative Thinking.* New York: G. P. Putnam's Sons, 1959.

II

The Nature of Teaching in the Creative Arts: Art

My definition, then, of the creative process is that it is the emergence in action of a novel relational product, growing out of the uniqueness of the individual on the one hand, the materials, events, people, or circumstances of his life on the other.[1]

CARL ROGERS

TO THE READER

Art expression is an obvious medium through which people create. Before you read this chapter, make a montage or try some sand molding as described on pages 74 and 84. After you finish your creation think through the process you followed. Does it compare with the steps children go through as described on page 5. Read this chapter and decide which factors entered into your creation which do not enter into the children's.

Introduction

What is art? In the teacher's guide to *Growing with Art,* Andrews and Ellsworth define it as follows:

Art is doing anything that needs to be done in the most beautiful way that it can be done. Art is a language of line, form, and color through which one may express feelings and attitudes. Art may be found in many activities, from the building of a cathedral to setting a table for breakfast or arranging arithmetic problems on a page. Art is the creative power of the human spirit. Art is not imitation. It is a personal response to a need or an experience.[2]

With a few minor changes, the above definition may also describe "What is music?" Extended it might also answer the questions, What is dance? What is drama? What is literature?

[1] Carl Rogers, "Toward a Theory of Creativity" in *Creativity and Its Cultivation,* ed. Harold Anderson (New York: Harper & Row, Publishers, Inc., 1959), p. 71.

[2] Maud Ellsworth and Michael F. Andrews, *Growing with Art:* A Teacher's Book (Syracuse: L. W. Singer Co., 1960), center pages.

. Just as children are capable of being more creative if they possess vast storehouses of knowledge and skills from which to draw, so can teachers be more creative when they possess a vast storehouse of knowledge about the subjects which they teach. This chapter will review some of the trends currently in vogue in the areas of the creative arts, with the exception of literature. The author feels strongly that literature written is one of the creative arts and literature read constitutes a major portion of a sound reading program, so he has devoted a discussion of the creative teaching of literature to another volume. The next two chapters will be confined to developing a viewpoint regarding art, music, dance and drama.

The Nature of Art

Art expression is one of the quickest ways a child shows his creative drives and it is found in many activities in a child's life, from the building of a toy house to the arrangement of a letter on a page. Creativity can be developed through art, but only if the concept of creativity is kept perpetually in mind. Teaching some kinds of so-called "art" can destroy creativity. *The basic goal of the teaching of art in the elementary school is to develop the creativity in children;* to help each child express himself in his own unique way.

Setting conditions for the creative teaching of art requires certain understandings:

1. To be creative, experiences in art must be open-ended. The teacher should place the child in situations where he is confronted with a problem which he can solve by using various art media. The giving of motivation and the teaching of necessary, convergent-thinking skills are in the realm of the teacher, but the child provides the solution of the problem, the consequent art product.

2. The teacher should strive for individuality and uniqueness; each art product should differ from all others. She must be very careful to remove patterns from children for patterns stilt their thinking, their working, and their ability to express themselves. Coloring books and reading exercises such as those where children "draw three balls like this" and "make a house like this and color it red" are discarded. The old technique of setting up a pattern of thinking in arithmetic such as, "We will look first for what is GIVEN, then

for what are we to FIND and then how will we SOLVE," must go. If the development of creativity gained through good art experiences is violated on the same day it is experienced, serious damage to the child's creative development will result.

3. The teacher should try to understand the processes involved in creating and not expect realism in the products. Very young children express themselves symbolically in many ways. Teachers encourage this in writing, reading and in using numbers but often reject symbolic expression in art—primarily because they do not understand it. Good painting is not true reproduction; the realm of true reproduction belongs to the photographer. But even photographers, with modern methods of developing, can fade out, enlarge or accent various areas of their pictures, thereby making a more artistic plate. It is the privilege of the artist to rearrange what he sees so he can express anything he desires, be it a mood, a feeling, a study of shade and light, a texture or a color study. Children at various stages of their growth enjoy making reproductions in their true form; boys at the age of ten or twelve draw comic strips and Disney characters with astonishing perfection. This is a child's way of practicing a skill. He is showing that he can make faces do what he wants them to; he can draw faces that laugh, bodies that run, planes that fly! His desire for detail on his planes and machines shows his sharpened sense of observation. This is the "drill" he gives himself in creating artistic trueness. It is possible that when a child reaches this stage, he may receive unnecessary amounts of praise for this type of reproduction over his abstract or creative representation, and because all children desire praise and status, he will gradually surrender his creative interpretation to reproduction. This is, in many instances, as far as he goes in art expression, for he becomes reliant on the way others express themselves and he has no place to go. He has not developed independent artistic expression so art is no longer a means of true expression for him. The teacher can encourage the imaginative expression of the child, while he has the urge to reproduce, so that he is able to proceed independently. Newfound techniques become an aid to greater individual effort and the child continues to grow independently.

The teacher must understand that children who reach the stages of communication in art where they desire to reproduce objects and people in their paintings as they see them, do so in various ways according to their development. A child cannot see the world through his teacher's eyes. In the process of growing up, he receives first

FIGURE 2–1. *A child readily learns to communicate through his painting. A four-year-old says, "This is me with a basket of oranges, and this is a butterfly and these are hornets flying from the tree."*

impressions of the world around him. For instance, after a trip to the zoo, a four-year-old made bold, black stripes across a sheet of paper and brought it to her Nursery School teacher. "Tell me about your painting," said the teacher.

"Why, it's a tiger at the zoo," said the four-year old in a tone that implied the teacher should have recognized it at once. The child was impressed by the bold color of the tiger's coat. She did not see the head, feet, tail and body in detail. Obviously she knew they were there, but this was not a new discovery to her. She painted what impressed her most.

When children first begin to paint people they omit the body and often draw the arms coming from the head where the ears should be. They are drawing what they see, though it is only an approximation of the truth. The child's head is very important to him; it enables him to talk, eat and smell. Often, he is more conscious of teeth than of the body, and draws faces in great detail before he gives his figure a body. Hands are important to the child so he draws hands with too many fingers. Legs and feet are also important so he often attaches

FIGURE 2–2. *A wide-eyed four-year-old said, "This is the tiger I saw at the zoo."*

them directly to the neck. It is only later, when he becomes conscious of his own body, that bodies appear in his drawings. Parents are often amazed that children draw teeth, nostrils, eyelashes and curls on their figures before drawing bodies. This is not so amazing if the parent can put himself in the child's place and realize that the observation powers of the child are constantly growing and changing. If adults would get on their knees and look up at other adults from the eye level of the child they would see how impressive the dark nostrils appear, and how noticeable are the teeth (especially gold ones that flash as an adult talks) and the blinking and flickering of the eyelashes.

The subject matter utilized in the young child's painting is largely his symbolic representation of the limited world around him. Children in the early communicative stages of art expression paint everything they see, or feel or like. Trips to the fire station or the post office provide the incentive for a wealth of active, exciting pictures by the children. People are also of great interest and they appear in the paintings. It is interesting to note the detail a child will put in a

FIGURE 2–3. *A four-year-old's attempt at drawing a man.*

feathered hat or a polka dot dress that impresses him, while the rest of the figure remains in very crude form.

The child's first reproductions of flowers, tables and people also lack trueness to size and perspective; as he looks up at objects he sees the undersides of objects which adults do not see. A child's perspective is different from the adult's. There is a point beyond which height is meaningless or distance makes little difference to the child. This is the child's means of comparison and must be accepted at this time as his true observations. He sees and thinks in terms of tall or small, tiny or great-big, long or short, not by inches and feet, height and weight, volume or area. Concepts develop slowly and as they develop he uses them in all forms of communication, including art expression, while constantly refining his ability to express himself.

So, the teacher should accept the child's trees, houses and flowers, though they may be all the same size. She should encourage the child to paint exactly what he feels and sees, for by doing so she helps him to develop his ability independently. As he grows and increases his observation and communication powers, the ability to reproduce objects exactly as he sees them becomes important only because he may use these reproductions in new and meaningful arrangements on paper. Children's paintings should be an interpretation of their own experiences and interests and not a random reproduction of visual impressions.

FIGURE 2–4. *When a child is so important in his world, his world is less important than himself.*

4. The teacher must recognize that the ability to express oneself through art is developmental. In his first encounter with new materials, the child experiments and explores. Lowenfeld identifies this stage as the non-schematic stage.[3] Later we begin to recognize some of the things the child paints; this is the schematic or communicative

---

[3] Viktor Lowenfeld, *Creative and Mental Growth* (New York: MacMillan Company, 1957).

stage. Still later, the child paints for the joy of painting; we call this the aesthetic stage.

Stages of growth in art expression must be considered as part of a developmental process and therefore temporary and experimental. Too much stress should not be placed on the permanency of children's paintings, for they often paint by the hour, discarding painting after painting. These paintings are experimental and the standards the child has set for himself may be lowered when a teacher insists on putting one on the bulletin board. To the child this may not be a finished product and for the teacher to praise it as such may discourage the child to go further in his experimentation. Just as drills on spelling words enable the child to better write stories and poems, so he needs the opportunity to explore and experiment through art media.

5. In order to set conditions for creative art experiences in the

FIGURE 2–5. *In the fifth grade you may discover perspective while painting the bridge.*

classroom, materials must be easily accessible. If children are to develop their use of art media, they must be given unlimited opportunity to experiment and explore. Locked cupboards do not provide incentive for frequent use of art materials. Art centers in classrooms should be equipped with easels, large tables for working and open shelves containing paints, crayons, various kinds of paper, paste, scissors and interesting scrap materials. Clay and plasticine, dyes, block prints, finger paint and other forms of artistic media add richness to the child's art experiences. Frequent opportunities should be planned for the children to use these materials and to apply them to bulletin board, flower and room arrangements.

6. A continual flow of stimuli must be present to encourage mental images which challenge the child to express himself through the media at hand. The subject matter at hand should vary with different age levels, for what a child paints is determined by his own development, his particular needs and interests or his own particular feelings. However, some subject matter (holidays for example) is common to all children and can be utilized for planned art lessons. Much of good art teaching, however, is on an individual basis, even when the interest is common. Following is a plan worked by one art teacher that illustrates the type of lesson that utilized a common interest, Lincoln's Birthday, yet fostered true creative effort on the part of each child.

A fifth grade class had asked to paint some pictures for Lincoln's Birthday. The results were a stereotyped silhouette pasted on the conventional white background. Realizing that a carry-over from former sterile art experiences had caused this, the art teacher set as her objective the problem of developing a creative experience from this very uncreative one.

Since creativity begins in the mind, the art teacher opened her lesson with a stimulation of the interests of the children to paint about Lincoln. She said:

"You know, when I think of Abraham Lincoln a whole flood of pictures comes to my mind. One of them I like very much. I see a tall, lanky, muscular young man in the middle of a clearing. He is stripped to the waist and he swings a gleaming axe in the sunlight as he splits rails for a fence. His legs are spread firmly apart and the sunlight makes ripples across his tanned body as the muscles flex with the movement of the gleaming axe. Behind him in the distance is a cabin with a thick spiral of smoke rising into the air. Behind that is the dark green forest. Above is the clear, blue sky, and in all that loneliness the sound of the axe is the only sound, the rippling of the man's body the only movement. What do you see when you think of Lincoln?"

One child raised his hand. "I see a long train draped with mourning and I see a band playing a funeral dirge. The train winds slowly in and out among the hills and stops at the towns where people stand, dressed in black along the way, sobbing. And the only color I see is the flags flapping at half-mast along the way."

Other children were catching the spirit. "I see a beautiful parade marching down Pennsylvania Avenue," said one boy. "There are bands playing and flags waving and thousands of people line the way and cheer. Lincoln is riding to the capitol. It is his inauguration day."

"I see a box in Ford's Theater—a torn flag hangs from the front of the box. A weary man clutches his side and falls forward over the torn flag. Mary Todd Lincoln stands gasping and the crowd below stares in terror at the sight of the man falling."

Each child who desired told what he saw and the panorama of the life of Lincoln unfolded itself and was painted verbally around the walls of the room in a riot of color, movement and form. Then it was but a step to transfer the verbal paintings to pictorial ones. The color, imagination and action which this simple discussion had released was a far cry from the row of black silhouettes along the front of the room.

There was one picture done in shocking blacks and purples, full of sadness and despair as the funeral train wound through the hills. The brightly painted flag and a few bits of colored bunting formed dramatic and startling contrasts. There was an action-filled picture of the muscular Mr. Lincoln in the sunlit field splitting rails. There was a picture of unbelievable sensitivity of Lincoln at the grave of Anne Rutledge.

The discussion of the paintings was an additional experience in thought-provoking communication. This was a creative experience to a great degree. There was some dependence on the art teacher, but she is here fulfilling her role well in taking the children from where they are and unfolding new possibilities for them while initiating a certain amount of freedom to work independently.

As the child grows older and his own world boundaries expand, he draws more and more of the things that interest him. Classroom units, holidays, special occurrences and exciting events often become

FIGURE 2–6. *A five-year-old realizes she may communicate with her paintings. Everybody knows it's the ears that make the rabbit!*

FIGURE 2–7. *She paints what she experiences directly.*

FIGURE 2–8. *She paints what she experiences vicariously.*

subjects of children's paintings. Boys in the intermediate grades draw airplanes, battleships, cowboys, astronauts with fantastic garb and Martian men. Girls of this age draw girl movie stars with long party dresses, ballet dancers and handsome men. They also like landscapes and pictures of foreign countries.

As the subjects of the child's painting change, so do his techniques and his abilities. Clay modeling is another form of art expression. Large painting as it is done on friezes and scenery for a play gives the child a different feeling toward space, area and paint. Sewing, weaving, fresco-painting and puppet-making all have their place in providing the child with creative outlets with wide and varied media. If these media are available most of the time in the classroom, some day the child will "discover" them and will also discover the techniques for using them. His joy at finding a new art expression will provide a motivation for his work with it.

One teacher helped provide new ideas through a classroom experience as follows:

The horizons of a fifth grade class were broadened for them when Shelly came to school. Shelly's father worked for a large American oil company, and every year the family spent December through March in Mexico. Along with many postal cards of Mexico, Shelly brought a serape, a sombrero, some lovely jewelry and glass and some dolls to school to show the children.

Immediately, she was confronted with a flood of questions. "Why are the hats so wide-brimmed?" "Why are the roofs of the desert houses flat?" "What is a serape used for?" Of course, every child was motivated to the point where a unit on Mexico became inevitable. The teacher saw tremendous possibilities for integrating all the children's work into lifelike situations and for incorporating many art experiences for the children. In the book on the Social Studies,[4] this unit is developed more fully, but some of its creative elements can be listed here to illustrate the rich experiences the children had as a result of their Mexican unit.

Some Experiences Arising From a Unit

1. The class read "The Painted Pig" and wrote a play from it.
   a. They made costumes for their play.

[4] James A. Smith, *Creative Teaching of the Social Studies in the Elementary School* (Boston: Allyn and Bacon, Inc., 1967).

b. They planned and painted scenery for their play.

c. They made properties for their play (Romona's tears strings, clay articles, wooden articles and cardboard articles).

d. They designed program covers and gave the play at a fiesta.

e. They made posters advertising the play.

2. The class drew and painted many pictures of Mexican life.

3. One committee made a large scrapbook for classroom reports and designed the cover.

4. The children gave a fiesta in the gymnasium to which they invited the entire school.

   a. Committees designed and built booths for displaying their materials on Mexico.

   b. Children planned exhibits of their paintings for the fiesta.

   c. Each child made a serape and sombrero to wear, using his own design.

   d. The children worked in papier-maché and created a life-size papier-mâché burro. He was used as an exhibit at the fair for the children's handmade wares.

   e. The class made Mexican pottery and tin jewelry to sell at the fair.

   f. The children did some weaving and tried other Mexican crafts.

   g. They decorated the gymnasium to represent a real Mexican plaza.

5. The class planned a program for the fiesta.

   a. They made Aztec masks and learned an ancient Aztec dance.

   b. They learned a Mexican hat dance and created costumes to wear while dancing.

   c. They learned songs in Spanish and English.

   d. They presented their play, "The Painted Pig."

6. The class served a Mexican meal.

   a. Each child made place mats with Mexican designs.

   b. Committees made centerpieces, based on the Mexican theme, for each table.

   c. The children made favors using Mexican designs.

7. The class had a Pinata Party.

   a. The children played Mexican games. One committee designed and made the Mexican pinata and filled it with gifts for all.

8. They dramatized a Mexican Christmas.

   a. The children made costumes and properties.

   b. The children created lighting effects for the Mexican procession to the nativity scene.

9. They studied Mexican art.

   a. A lecturer from Mexico visiting a neighboring town came and talked to the children and showed them many Mexican paintings and handicrafts.

   b. Children studied Mexican artists and found reproductions of their painting for bulletin board exhibits.

   c. The children studied Spanish architecture and found buildings in town with Spanish influence.

    d. They studied the ancient Aztec Indians and made masks for the Aztec dance at the fiesta.

10. They gave puppet plays.
    a. Many Mexican stories were read and hand puppets and marionettes were used to dramatize the stories.

11. The children studied Mexican music.
    a. They learned songs in Spanish.
    b. They listened to Spanish recordings.
    c. They studied and heard recordings of the opera "Carmen" and eventually went to see it.

These art experiences were possible only because the children were skillfully introduced to a whole new world and were allowed to experience the things connected with this world.

7. The teacher must provide a permissive atmosphere and a "level of expectancy" in the classroom which will keep the children experimenting, producing and discovering. She should use as many of the natural experiences of children as possible in promoting art expression but she should also set up situations to provoke their imaginations to go beyond the realm of the ordinary and she will develop the creative thinking which results in creative expression.

The teacher must realize that, at certain stages, the best teaching may be no teaching at all. She must develop a sensitivity to that psychological moment when she will withdraw from the situation leaving the child to summon his resources and fulfill the creative act on his own.

Teachers often express doubts concerning their ability to teach art because they cannot draw well themselves, but often teachers who cannot draw well do a better job of teaching young children than those who can. Their standards are not high and they are likely to leave the children to their own devices. The child is free to explore, manipulate and experience to his heart's content. This is perhaps the most important technique for teaching—that the child have materials to work with and a chance to try them out. The teacher at this point should recognize the child's purpose in painting and not demand finished products of him. She should show interest in the child's painting by asking that he tell about it—not by asking what it is supposed to be.

Children have a natural sense of color, harmony and balance. The teacher needs to encourage the growth of the child's ability to relate objects and produce good art principles in his pictures. She does not stop to teach a formal lesson on perspective, or to teach

FIGURE 2–9. *"Feel" the dancing.*

FIGURE 2–10. *Sing in the native tongue.*

FIGURE 2–11. *Create from experience.*

balance, but helps the child to sharpen his sense of observation and discover these things for himself.

A child who is attempting to say things with his paint brush may become irritated when the brush fails to say what he wants it to say. He paints his chimney jutting from the roof at a ninety degree angle and senses it is incorrect, yet by himself he cannot discover the technique for painting it correctly. He does not "see" why he is really painting it incorrectly. A repeated series of such experiences may cause him to surrender the art experience for a more successful one. Repeated failures may result in a disinterested attitude in art expression. The teacher can play an important part in resolving this failure experience and thus guide the child to a successful experience and on to another step. She may note his problem and step to the window, pointing out that the line of the side of the house across the street goes the same way as the line of the chimney. The child can try again with his sharpened observation and new knowledge to communicate the true picture that has suddenly become so important to him.

The technique is similar to that in all good teaching. In reading, for instance, the teacher can show the child a technique for tackling the pronunciation of a new word or tell him the word at once. The danger in art teaching lies not in showing, telling or providing techniques but in showing the child *what* to make, thus submerging his own ideas. Techniques are necessary for the final attainment of his own creative idea. They should be acquired quickly so they do not hinder him in his accomplishment. The ones he does not learn through self-discovery, manipulation or explanation, the teacher should help him to learn.

As the child progresses to the middle grades and becomes more conscious of his own planned art products and more sensitive to the aesthetic values of his art work, the teacher can help him develop his knowledge of art principles by encouraging their discovery on his part. In painting a forest scene for a play or in making a painting, perspective can be discovered by suggesting to children that they "put trees behind each other," or that they "fill in the background." Children develop a feeling for depth as well as a sense of perspective when they think about perspective this way.

Barbara, a fifth grader, was trying to paint a road going over a hill. She could not make the path look as though it wound over the hill. She tried and tried but always the path seemed stuck on the foreground of the picture. The teacher suggested Barbara make her brush walk over the hill like the road would go. In a matter of

FIGURE 2–12. *A seven-year-old reproduces his impressions of a baseball player.*

seconds she was painting bold strokes in the foreground and dainty strokes in the background as the road went over the hill. Wide-eyed and excited about discovering a new technique, Barbara turned to teacher and exclaimed, "That does it! What a terrific idea!"

Children who need help in developing a sense of balance can be urged to "fill the page," or "make things fit." The focus of interest can be developed by asking "Where should my eyes rest?" and then, "Do they?" Children can be encouraged to relate objects in their paintings by the simple suggestion, "Can we tie them together so they seem to belong to each other?" It is sometimes helpful for a teacher to suggest a technique to help a child, such as: "If the sun were shining on the left, wouldn't there be more light on this side?", or "It would be better if the background were not quite so busy. Can you make it quieter?" Suggestions such as this, when the child is ready for them, and when held to a minimum, can help the child to experiment and discover for himself. While he works efficiently with some techniques he has perfected he is always exploring and discovering new ones.

A teacher's role varies with the maturation of the child. In the early ages she provides an environment rich in materials and ideas and a permissive atmosphere so the child is free to explore, manipulate and discover. In the early intermediate grades, the teacher provides more guidance, helps the child discover new techniques and motivates him by use of a rich environment full of many ideas and suggestions. Much of the vocabulary of art technique can be mastered as children begin to evaluate their own work. The teacher can encourage and promote art for art's sake, she can provide children with many techniques and an opportunity to carry them out, she can develop art principles and art standards through experience and discussion.

The uses of art can be promoted most effectively at this intermediate level. Art should be used for solving problems created by classroom work. Scrapbook covers, scenery for plays and puppet shows, murals, Christmas cards, posters, program covers and a variety of activities may all be the result of children's attempts to solve problems through the use of art media. These children learn through experience to make their pictures fit a space, to adapt media for a purpose and to enrich through direct application the common experiences of everyday life. A direct consciousness of art principles can be developed readily through a wise use of these activities.

One fifth grade class wrote a play called *The Adventures of Robin Hood* as an outgrowth of a social studies unit. As the unit unfolded, the class decided to present the play for the rest of the school and the parents. It was agreed that posters were needed to advertise the play. Some individuals in the class agreed to make posters and during the work period two or three were made. When the class reported on their work at the end of the period, the posters were shown. In a classroom where a good social climate exists and children frequently evaluate themselves and the group, work of this kind can be judged in the right spirit and children can build their own standards. One of the children remarked that, from where he was sitting, he could not read the poster. Another child stated that the paint used on the poster seemed too light; the picture was not easily seen from the rear of the group. Still another felt the poster would look better if the lettering were more even.

A discussion followed and the class reviewed the purposes of

FIGURE 2–13. *Holidays can inspire creative interpretations.*

posters and made suggestions for making good posters. The following chart resulted and was used as a standard check list for making posters.

THINGS TO REMEMBER
ABOUT MAKING POSTERS

1. It is attractive?
2. It is neat?
3. Does it tell something?
   a. The event
   b. The time
   c. The place
   d. The price
   e. Other important information
4. Is the lettering neat?

5. Does it have one thing more important than others, made so by color, size or position?
6. Does this one thing catch your attention at once?
7. Do you look the second time for the important information?
8. Is it artistic?

This example provides a good sample of the deferred judgment technique explained in Chapter I.

A teacher may show the children how to make *papier-mâché* for puppets, but the children themselves can discover many ways for constructing the puppets and their own puppets will vary in structure and design. One class held a discussion on ways they could make marionette legs and bodies. Several methods were suggested:

> rolling paper and pasting it
> wetting and rolling masking tape
> using papier-mâché
> cutting them from wood
> sewing cloth forms and stuffing them
> using plastic wood

Each child proceeded to make his puppet in his own way. Approximate size was determined by the class and then the children were left to their own resources. There was great variation in the finished puppets—each child experimented with the use of many materials from the scrap box. They made hair by using paint, cut crepe paper, unbraided rope, yarn, steel wool, string, loopers, artificial hair and braided cloth. They made eyes from paint, buttons, beads, tacks, "glitter," cut paper and enamel. Each aspect of the building of the puppets called for creative thinking on the part of the children and the results were unique and individual. Children learn from each other and challenge each other to new creative efforts.

8. The teacher should develop a sensitivity to beauty—an aesthetic sense.

The classroom itself should be not only a workshop but also a place where objects of beauty, made by the children, will be displayed and appreciated.

The truly lovely paintings of the past and the creations of the present are all part of a child's rightful heritage; the child is able to evaluate, interpret and learn from them. The more contact he has with paintings of all kinds, the more adept he becomes at building his own standards and enjoying his own culture.

Many teachers feel children's techniques and paintings are influenced and restricted when other paintings are set before them. The desire to copy tends to reduce the child's own attempt to think and paint creatively. Carried to excess, this can be true. But children who have frequently experienced the joy of creating in many ways are interested in observing how others create. They paint when they have something to say and are not eager to copy other people's work. They may, however, borrow ideas and accumulate techniques for building standards of original expression and skilled workmanship.

Art objects and fine paintings should be used in the classroom. The teacher should choose the subjects according to the age level and the interests of the children. She should draw attention to the pictures, discuss them with the children and acquaint them with the artist.

A fourth grade was discussing a beautiful winter scene which the teacher had borrowed from a nearby college picture library for a week. Paul said, "You know, Miss Perkins, the artist really painted the snow green but it looks white." Some of the children doubted the snow was green so Paul cut a hole in a piece of paper and placed it over the rest of the painting so that only an area of the snow showed through. It was green! An excellent discussion followed on ways to get effect through use of color. Many children, looking out of the window, pointed out the fact that the snow outside really was quite blue on this day and the shadows cast by the tiny hills were almost purple. This class had made an exciting discovery and a whole period of investigating and exploring with their own paints resulted.

This teacher was using a good painting wisely. Children enjoy knowing the stories of paintings also. They thrill to Raphael's "Madonna of the Chair" and the story of its creation. Stories about pictures are best told after the children have had an opportunity to enjoy the aesthetic qualities of the picture, so their pleasure comes from the painting as well as the association connected with it.

To see a child copying occasionally is not a matter over which a teacher should become alarmed. Children often teach themselves a new technique or perfect an old one by copying someone else's craftsmanship for a while. It is only when this work replaces a child's own expression that a teacher needs to feel concern.

Most normal boys and girls at the ages of ten to twelve find keen delight in reproducing the comics. Much of this is consistent with their development. They are reaching the age where they like to master their work, and in their art expression, they want to master trueness. These boys and girls turn out copies of Mickey Mouse, Superman, movie stars, copied drawings of books and stereotyped profiles on a mass production basis. The teacher's job here is one of encouraging them to employ their new-found technique in new creative ways.

Buddy, a fifth grader, stopped his own creative attempts for a period of three weeks while he copied Disney characters by the score. While in and out of school he drew Disney's creations to the finest detail and with increasing accuracy. For a while he became the center of admiration of the group.

The teacher utilized some of this talent by inspiring Buddy to make posters for the play, "Snow White and the Seven Dwarfs," which the second grade was to give. Meanwhile she searched for new ways to help Buddy develop his own creative ideas with his newly-developed abilities. One day the opportunity presented itself. The class was publishing a newspaper and at the staff meeting Bruce suggested they have more cartoons. Buddy immediately volunteered to draw a weekly comic strip of Mickey Mouse. At first the class was enthusiastic. Teacher, seizing her opportunity, said, "I think the idea of a weeky comic strip is excellent. However, I wonder if it is wise for us to 'steal' someone else's idea for our paper. After all, Mickey Mouse is Walt Disney's invention. Walt Disney thought him up in his mind and made him famous. Have we a right to use his idea this way?"

In the discussion that followed, Olive, age 10, brought up the fact that Mickey Mouse was also a copyrighted feature and by law we had no right to reproduce it. Bobby suggested they make up their own comic strip.

As a result, Buddy came forth the next week with a whole new string of ideas in a comic strip, "The Adventures of Doodles Duck." For weeks, new characters of fearful and wonderful proportions and personalities appeared to delight the children.

Other people's art products should be used in the classroom just as should other people's compositions, poems and stories. Feelings and ideas can be effectively communicated through art media to children. Good teaching involves many experiences of this sort and a good teacher takes her pupils to museums, art galleries, good films, concerts and beautiful community homes to develop empathy with the creative spirit and to give her children an appreciation of the creativity of others.

9. Continuous effort on the teacher's part should be made to

help each child develop his creative ability, though the abilities of individual children may vary widely. On occasion, disturbed children or children who appear to have lost their individuality need special help in rediscovering their own abilities. In such instances it is necessary for the teacher to focus careful attention on those conditions which will free this child from his inhibitions. Setting up these conditions may necessitate the use of unusual methods to gain creative art expression.

Oddly enough, the very measures through which the creative power of the child has been dimmed may be utilized to recapture those powers. In art experiences, for example, copying or tracing patterns may have restricted the child's interpretation and observation. In order to lead a child away from the concept that his art product is a good one if it closely resembles a pattern or is a replica of someone else's work, the teacher may first encourage the child to make his traced Christmas tree or his turkey *different* from that of the other children. Soon his individuality begins to assert itself in many small ways and, if encouraged, will perhaps grow. This will not often be a quick change, for this child has to unlearn; the teacher must re-teach, which is much more difficult than teaching.

If the child has had the greatest of all his abilities killed, his creative ability, almost any step the teacher takes to reawaken that ability is legitimate if it results in a richer life for the child. Deprived of his creative powers, a child has lost one of his finest techniques of communication. Such a child is not equipped for a full satisfactory life; he has no way of deriving pleasure from what he has and from what nature has provided him; he seeks pleasure and satisfaction outside himself, never realizing that the greatest satisfactions and pleasures he can find lie within himself and in his own inherent ability to create his own happiness. Our world is filled with people of this sort and the schools of our culture cannot afford to turn out more like them.

The Role of the Specialist

What is the place of the art or music teacher in the emerging elementary school where creativity is recognized as an inherent potential in all individuals and where an understanding of the creative process does not limit it to an art or music period? The talents of specialists in this new setting are often wasted by overloading them with tightly packed schedules which makes their work ineffectual or even damaging to a good elementary schoolroom program. To attempt to put a special teacher in each classroom for a few periods during a school week is a waste of time and energy in terms of value received. The main contributions of special teachers do not lie in teaching tricks to children in a hurried half hour visit to the classroom. Such isolated experiences are entirely divorced from the rest of the child's classroom activities. In some instances even the regular teacher regards these visits as free time and leaves the room for a rest or utilizes the period as a chance to correct papers or to finish other classroom chores. The experience is apt to have little or no meaning to many children, in terms of developing creativity.

If programs such as those discussed in this book are to be followed, and if the objectives concerning the development of creativity are to be attained, the development of each child is of primary importance. A classroom teacher studies her children, she knows the problems of each and she plans steps to help him. She watches his behavior change; she sees him maturing in attitude, she understands his faults and his strengths. She works with the child's parents to make him a better-adjusted individual. It is reasonable to hope that the classroom teacher will guide each experience the child has so that he will approach his potential.

A special teacher who goes from room to room cannot be expected to know every child in a school. Under time pressures, she is generally more concerned with teaching an art or music lesson than with developing creativity in children. Some can handle this with skill but most become so burdened that their visits only isolate art from everyday life; the children enjoy art periods, not because they are rich and creative, but because they are a relief from the humdrum of school life.

The above situation does not employ school resources to their full potential. Creativity is not something that can be turned on and off like a spigot. Children faced with a task beyond their ability, or forced to create while in an uncreative mood, can only acquire poor attitudes and frustrations about art and music. Often damage is done to the individual or to a lesson carefully planned by the classroom teacher.

The classroom teacher should assume the responsibility for teaching everything that goes on in her classroom. She alone knows her pupils and her objectives and her plans should include experiences which help her meet those objectives. Isolated experiences conducted by strangers are usually only slightly valuable and should not constitute the only creative experiences children have in their school life.

In other areas a specialist diagnoses and prescribes, while trained personnel carry out his prescription. It should be thus for the specialist in the school. Attempting to teach each child in a school system is an exhausting and unnecessary experience for specialists in the creative arts. A more fruitful program would utilize these people as other professions utilize their specialists: for providing training and help for those who are not so highly specialized and/or for use as consultant when special help is needed.

A specialist can bring to a staff new ideas concerning the teaching of creative arts. He can help teachers develop their own creative abilities by providing rich opportunities for them to explore and utilize creative materials. In some schools, staff meetings, held on afternoons after an early dismissal of the children, are sometimes utilized for art, music and physical education workshops where the specialists teach the teachers. They, in turn, return to their classrooms and teach their boys and girls. Programs such as these deploy the energy of the specialist into channels where everyone may benefit. They are economic in terms of time expenditure and keep a school staff constantly informed, stimulated, united and secure in the steps it takes toward meeting its objectives. Obviously such a spirit affects the children and promotes better educational programs, rich with satisfying social experiences.

In some schools teachers invite the specialists to help plan units of work. They sit down with the music, art and physical education teachers and go over their plans with them, asking for suggestions for including creative experiences in their work. In this way many ideas are shared and the specialists discover where they can help the teacher and when they will be needed to help teacher and pupils. They can also share materials with this teacher and learn from her about the children who need special help.

The teacher comes to a place in her plans where she has neither the ability nor the equipment to proceed alone. Rather than halt her children's progress, she seizes an opportunity for them to meet and work with new personalities, and through careful planning, the specialist acts as a consultant in helping the children solve their problems. The specialist does not necessarily take over the class, but works in a team teaching situation with the classroom teacher. These periods can fit into the specialist's schedule and still enable him to spend his energies where they are most needed. A class studying transportation may wish to do a wall frieze on what they have learned and may need the help of an art teacher for several days. After this experience they may not need the art teacher again for several weeks. It is only when many classes demand his time simultaneously that it becomes necessary for him to organize his program to the point where he can apportion his time most effectively.

Very careful use of the consultant's time was worked out in one school. Each consultant put a mimeographed time schedule on the wall outside the door of his office, blocking each day into hour long periods. When a problem arose where the teacher and children of a particular classroom felt that they needed the help of the special teacher, they would determine the day and length of time they might need him and dispatch a committee to sign up for that time. If that time was not available, the next best was chosen. The specialist was obtained when and where he was most needed and could adjust his teaching to the needs and interests of the group. Before each visit, the classroom teacher contacted him and briefed him on the purpose of his visit and advised him on what he could do for the children. In this way each experience with the specialist was a valuable one, fitting in with the regular activity of the group and contributing toward reaching the teacher's goals.

Wise use of the specialist's time can be worked out in many areas, namely: science, shop, home economics or reading. The specialist must be cautious to reserve time to visit the classroom to study the children to determine areas where he might provide guidance and help to the teacher. This sort of relationship calls for and builds high professional attitudes among staff members. The specialist himself must be a creative person who understands and enjoys people and who will not impose himself but will apply his specialized skill, technique or point of view when they are needed.

One of the greatest criticisms of the popular trend toward team teaching is that in many instances one teacher takes over a class for a while and there is little or no continuity in the program between members of the team. Any administrative plan is doomed to failure when subject matter has priority over children. Real team teaching means that *many* people come to know the children well; the team does a better job in developing creative abilities than a single teacher can do. Otherwise, the whole idea defeats its own purpose.

Experience and Application

Creating means producing something new, unique and individual. In art this means using familiar media in new ways. To develop creativity through art the teacher must keep two things in mind: (1) she must constantly expose children to new materials and help them understand the qualities of these new materials and (2) she must provide unique situations and problems in her classroom to which these new materials may be applied.

Children may be introduced to new materials by direct use as well as through class discussion. A kindergartener best learns about the qualities of finger paint by finger painting, but a sixth grader may discuss and explore the use of grout without actually using it artistically. The teacher will, of course, want to set conditions soon after this discussion where grout might be used to solve a problem so children can experience its use. Learning about the qualities of many materials provides children with the necessary background for using those materials in creative ways.

When the new school building opened, the children were delighted upon seeing the beautiful mosaic in the hall. Charlie asked how they managed to keep all those little pieces of glass together. The art teacher brought in some tiles and some grout and demonstrated the process. No attempt was made to create a design or a pattern; the children simply explored the qualities of the materials. Many children became interested enough to work with mosaics and all the children learned about the use of grout.

Not long after this experience, the teacher confronted the children with a problem: What could they use to cover an old table she had found to make it attractive, stain-proof and durable? The children were planning to use this table in their reading center.

"What materials do we know of which would be suitable for this purpose?" the teacher asked.

The children listed these materials which would not easily stain and which would be attractive:

1. hard finish enamel paint
2. a design covered with glass
3. rubber tiles

4. varnish
5. shellac
6. contact paper

Charlie said, "What about making a tile design like the wall in the foyer? We learned how to use grout the other day!"

The experiences suggested on the following pages were chosen with two purposes in mind: (1) to acquaint children with the qualities of a variety of materials and (2) to create situations where a variety of materials may be put to creative use.

The creative teacher, herself, will need to experience the use of many materials and know their qualities in order to lead the children forward in an effective manipulation of their environment.

The illustrations described in Chapter IV were chosen to show teachers how children produced creatively after they have learned the qualities of many materials. In each instance a problem was presented and the children helped determine the materials most suitable for solving it. Although readers may want to pose similar problems to their students, the children may come up with completely different results than those described here.

Summary

To develop creativity through the use of art media, the teacher should provide many open-ended problem situations which can be expressed through the use of a variety of art materials. She should strive for individuality in the products which result as a solution to those problems and strive for both realism and expression through design and color. Understanding that the development of children plays a large part in their ability to work with art media, the teacher should provide many materials which are easily accessible for children and perpetuate a flow of stimuli to continually motivate them. Art activity should be promoted in her classroom by maintaining a permissive atmosphere and a level of expectancy. She should develop a sensitivity to beauty, and constantly expose children to new media, teach them new skills and techniques and help them to discover basic art principles.

The classroom teacher and the art teacher must work with the same goals and objectives in mind if creativity is to be conscientiously developed in each child. Both must integrate their teachings in a comprehensive program of creative art and child development.

TO THE COLLEGE STUDENT

1. What feelings do you associate with your elementary school art and music periods? Try to analyze them. Take a class consensus of these feelings. Does your class reaction come out anything like that of the class mentioned in the Preface of this book? Who taught the creative arts in your school? What kind of person was she? Did she follow the basic principles in this chapter? Do you think she helped to develop your own creativity? How?

2. Think of a popular college event such as Spring Weekend, the Junior Prom, a major football game, a festival of arts or a great dramatic production. Divide your class into five groups. Have one group interpret the weekend through painting, one through dance, one through pantomime, one through dramatization and one through music. Present your ideas to each other.

3. Make a list of all the techniques you have seen teachers use that void creativity in the creative arts.

4. Following is a list of quotes overheard by the author in recent classroom observations he has made. Decide which ones encouraged creative development and which ones discouraged it.

"I told you to cut the leaf to the edge of the paper. Now it will be too small and won't look like the others on the bulletin board."

"That doesn't look like a log to me—where are the lines which show the bark?"

"I told you to be careful not to cut outside the lines!"

"Listen to Molly's tune—she has an idea which is different from any others."

"Bill, I never saw a lumberman chop like that!"

"Helen, I think you are not acting like a doormouse should act."

"Children, look at what Bill is doing—does that help to give the idea that he is a dormouse?"

5. A college student has been unjustly accused of cheating on an exam and has been called to the professor's office. To free himself of suspicion would mean placing the blame on a fraternity brother. Role-play the scene in the instructor's office. After five minutes have

the players reverse roles and play the same scene and note what happens.

TO THE CLASSROOM TEACHER

1. Examine the art, music and physical education programs at your school. Do you know what goes on in each of these programs or do you leave the room during these periods? Do you and the specialists supplement each other as a team or do you each work separately? How can you develop a more united program for the development of creativity in the children?

2. Think through the ways you void creative development when you do not work with the special teachers in planning integrated work for the children.

3. How could you use your specialists to enrich a unit you are currently teaching?

4. How many ways could you use the creative arts to enrich your daily program besides having regular art, music or physical education periods?

TO THE COLLEGE STUDENT AND
THE CLASSROOM TEACHER

1. Plan a classroom which will be a laboratory for learning in the creative arts.

2. Make collections from the paintings of your pupils which do not have meaning to you but which obviously mean something to the child.

3. Collect paintings for display which obviously show the stages of art development in the children: non-schematic, schematic, communicative, representative, aesthetic.

4. Discuss this statement: "Teaching art for art's sake and music for music's sake is developing creativity in children."

5. Make lists of all the unusual media that might be introduced to children for creative development. Think of media not mentioned

in this chapter such as colored sand for sand painting, colored sawdust, ceramic tile, colored glass, etc.

6. Look through the samples of children's paintings in this chapter and classify them under the following categories: (1) non-schematic, (2) schematic, (3) representative or communicative, (4) aesthetic.

7. List all the art, music, dramatic and dance experiences which could be incorporated in a unit on rockets.

8. Think of all the specific instances you can where "the best teaching may be no teaching at all" in the creative arts (see page 30).

SELECTED BIBLIOGRAPHY

ANDERSON, WARREN H. *Art Learning Situations for Elementary Education*. Belmont: Wadsworth Publishing Co., Inc., 1966.

ASSOCIATION FOR SUPERVISION AND CURRICULUM DEVELOPMENT. *Perceiving, Behaving, Becoming*. Washington, D.C.: National Education Association, 1962.

BARKAN, MANUEL. *Through Art to Creativity*. Boston: Allyn and Bacon, Inc., 1960.

COLE, NATALIE R. *The Arts in the Classroom*. New York: John Day Co., 1940.

CONRAD, GEORGE. *The Process of Art Education in the Elementary School*. Englewood Cliffs: Prentice-Hall, Inc., 1964.

COSNER, E. I. "What Is Creativity in the Curriculum?" *Middle School*, LXXV (1960), 22–23.

DUNKEL, H. B. "Creativity and Education," *Education Theory*, XI (1960), 209–16.

GUILFORD, J. P. "Creative Abilities in the Arts," *Psychological Review*, LXIV (1957), 110–18.

KAGAN, PAULINE W. *From Adventure to Experience Through Art*. San Francisco: Chandler Publishing Company, 1959.

LASSWELL, H. D. "The Social Setting of Creativity," in H. Anderson, ed., *Creativity and Its Cultivation*. New York: Harper & Row, Publishers, Inc., 1959.

LOWENFELD, VICTOR. *Creative and Mental Growth*. New York: MacMillan Co., 1947.

MEAD, MARGARET. *A Creative Life for Your Children*. Washington: U.S. Department of Health, Education and Welfare, 1962.

REED, E. G. *Developing Creative Talent*. New York: Vantage Press, Inc., 1962.

RUBIN, L. J. "Creativity and the Curriculum," *Phi Delta Kappan,* XLIV (1963), 438–40.

RUSSELL, DAVID. *Children's Thinking.* New York: Blaisdell Publishing Co., 1956.

VEATCH, JEANETTE. "The Structure of Creativity," *Journal of Educational Psychology,* XXVII (1953), 102–7.

WILT, MARION E. *Creativity in the Elementary School.* New York: Appleton-Century-Crofts, Inc., 1959.

WOLFSON, B. J. "Creativity in the Classroom," *Elementary English,* XXXVIII (November 1961), 523.

ZIRBES, LAURA. *Spurs to Creative Teaching.* New York: G. P. Putnam's Sons, 1959.

The Nature of Teaching in the Creative Arts: Music, Dance and Dramatics

Musical training is a more potent instrument than any other, because rhythm and harmony find their way into the inward places of the soul.[1]

PLATO

TO THE READER

Your author recently visited a fourth grade classroom where the children had been studying Indians. They had listed the names of the following tribes on the chalkboard: Choctaw, Chickasaw, Cherokee, Cree, Iroquois, Seneca and Comanchee.

When one young fellow started to read them off, he exclaimed with the joy of discovery, "Hey, you can't read those names like that —you have to sing them!"

His discovery resulted in a delightful song composed of the names of the Indian tribes.

Read the lines again and see what he meant. Add to them and create an Indian Song of your own.

The Nature of Music

Music has always been one of man's best-known methods of communication. It has often been called the only existing international language. Through the use of music man has been able to express his feelings so that other men can understand him. The unique qualities of each culture have been captured in music and transmitted to the peoples of other cultures.

From the time a baby is able to hear distinctly, he responds to the music from the radio or phonograph which plays in his room. He coos or shakes the slats in his crib or playpen or moves his body up and down in an uneven rhythm. If he has a springy chair or a swing, he bounces up and down to the rhythm of the music. He soon learns to hum little tunes and often beats his rattle, spoon or toys against the

[1] Plato, *The Republic:* Book I.

side of his high chair in an unplanned yet distinct rhythm. This is all part of the creative drive within him and his desire for rhythmical experiences. There is rhythm in the baby's creeping, in the noises he makes and later in his walking. There is rhythm in dancing, in baking a cake, in playing games, in breathing, in swimming, in working on the assembly line. This rhythm, when patterned and planned, becomes musical expression.

There are two objectives to be kept in mind when teaching music:

1. to help children develop their own creative powers through music.
2. to help children live enriched lives by meeting their need for musical experiences and help them to develop an appreciation and love of good music by promoting an understanding of what the composer is trying to say.

Music as a tool to develop creativity has not been used as much in our schools as it has been used for pure enjoyment. But music can provide ways of developing creativity comparable to art if it is utilized frequently. A child who has experienced the joy of hearing his composition played or sung by his classmates is not only expressing himself creatively but he is also well on the way to meeting objective two. As a person who paints appreciates other paintings better, so does a person who composes appreciate others' compositions better.

Too often music is taught by a music teacher who blindly selects the songs and the skills which are to be taught without regarding the needs, interests or readiness of the children. They often associate unpleasant memories with music experiences of this sort and they soon form attitudes toward music that are opposed to the objectives for including music in the school program. Music is best taught by using the equipment the child possesses and leading him forward, not by imposition of teacher's standards.

Children are frequently expected to attain musical perfection in learning a song or playing an instrument and this is often impossible for them. As in art, they need to spend much of their time exploring, manipulating and perfecting techniques so that they can better communicate musically. They will do this by the hour if given the opportunity. Here again, the thrill of discovering what they can do becomes a great motivating technique for children. Too much copying of other people's work and not enough experimenting on his own may soon discourage the child and hold in check his own desire to explore his

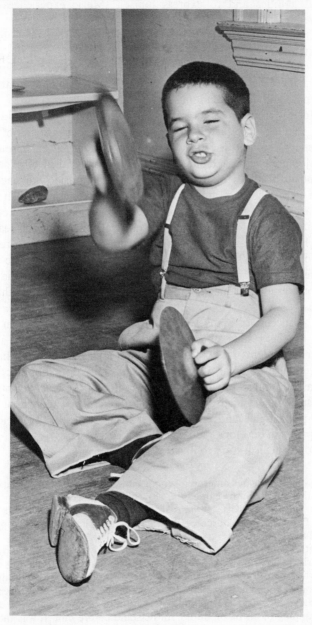

FIGURE 3–1. *There is much to discover about music, and the crash of cymbals makes you squint with anticipation.*

musical abilities and to express himself. Music experiences to be creative must be open-ended.

Children love to know and sing many songs, but they also love to create their own. Simple, one-line songs by children in the kindergarten should be regarded as the product of the ability of the five-year-old, and the necessary drill he needs to be better able, at a later age, to compose and understand music.

Musical readiness is as important as reading readiness. Just as a child's reading powers rely to a degree on a background of social experiences, so do his musical powers rest on a background of musical experiences. A child who has had a great deal of experience with music becomes ready for more difficult music with each successive step. He hears music a great deal, makes up his own songs, and learns to sing the songs of others. Then, later he is ready to recognize that " ♩ " can represent a musical tone. He soon learns to record his own musical creations and eventually he learns to read the music of others. When children are forced into reading music before they are ready, poor attitudes, accompanied by a dislike for the music situation, result. This negative feeling for music may persist throughout life.

The success of many school music programs is too often determined by the results obtained at a school concert where a large number of students take part in singing, playing in a school band or displaying instrumental accomplishments. This does not necessarily imply a good music program. The true value of the teaching program can best be determined by the extent to which *each* individual in the school participates and enjoys music and the degree to which the music program develops each child's creative powers.

Following is a story to illustrate the above:

A visiting teacher entered a school building on a day near Christmas. From the auditorium came the lovely strains of children's voices singing Christmas carols. He paused, carried away by the sweetness of the voices. Drawn to the source of the heavenly music, he pushed open the auditorium doors.

Before him, in the darkened assembly, only the stage was lighted. About sixty children of ten to twelve years of age stood singing on the stage while before them, in the orchestra pit, the music teacher directed them and another teacher played the piano. This picture card scene was soon shattered by an abrupt halt of the conductor's movements and an angry rapping of his baton on the music stand before him. It was then that the visitor noticed the frightened look on the faces of the children, the tenseness of their bodies, the wistful glances from their eyes toward the podium. The conductor proceeded to scream at the children, calling them stupid and threatening to keep them all day until they sang the carol correctly. Some anxious children trembled, those who were more secure would have smiled if they dared, all stood taut and tense while they received their verbal beating. After the irate teacher had calmed himself, they were told to try it again—this time with *no* mistakes. Again the heavenly music floated forth.

The teacher was striving for a finished product; what happened to the children in the process was of little consequence. One cannot help but wonder what pressures were being placed on him which made him treat the children in such a manner. Just what this teacher hoped to achieve by his exhibition is impossible to comprehend. Certainly none of the objectives of education were being met.

As soon as we set perfection as our goal, our real purpose in teaching music is lost. We should not be attempting to develop musicians in our children, but we should be releasing musical expression and building good attitudes toward musical communication.

The best evaluation of any music program is not how well each child can sing or play but (1) does each child approach the music experience with anticipation and joy, (2) does he love music and (3) does the music experience contribute to his creative development?

The Nature of Rhythms and Dance

Rhythms, properly used, can lead to another form of creative outlet —the dance. Communication can take place among people through bodily movement as well as through verbalism or visual aids. Rhythms are sometimes encouraged in the kindergarten and first grades and are then forgotten until the child reaches adolescence and desires to participate in social dancing. This is unfortunate, for the years between kindergarten and junior high school are the growth years, when the child needs help in moving gracefully and reassurance that he is handling his body correctly. Many times his awkwardness is accented rather than diminished when he takes dancing lessons and is forced into a "one-two-three" pattern. Children cannot handle such instruction with ease because the movements of their growing bodies are difficult to control.

The dance, in order to be creative, must be considered in different terms than those commonly affiliated with it. Dance should not be taught in the type of class where all children do the same thing at the same time and follow fixed patterns of movement predetermined by the dancing teacher. This method has no place in the initial training of dance, but it should come after the children have had the opportunity to create their own dances. Once they have experienced free dance movement, established a relationship to space and mastered the concept of dance patterns, learning a fox trot, a waltz or a tap dance is a fairly simple matter.

People everywhere have danced to express feeling and to communicate ideas. A natural expression of the inborn creative drive of every individual, dance plays a more dominant role in our own civilization with each passing year. Chapter V of this book develops the concept of the school dance program as it relates to creative development.

FIGURE 3–2. *All ages enjoy folk dancing.*

The Nature of Creative Dramatics

Creative dramatics affords another means of developing creative expression in elementary school children. Because dramatization is closely allied to reading, literature and the language arts, the author has developed the philosophy behind creative dramatics and has given several examples of its use, in Books II and III of this series. Something remains to be said, however, regarding the creative teaching of dramatics as a means of developing creativity.

Too often the teaching of dramatics in the elementary school is confined to its interpretative function rather than its creative function. Children enjoy dramatizing nursery rhymes, stories and poems at an early age and most of their learning takes place in the early years through the basis of all dramatization—mimicry. Mimicry, a form of interpretation, can be creative in many respects but if it is employed excessively as the main utilization of dramatics to creative development, the chances for developing creative powers through this media narrow as the child progresses through his school years.

Like that of art, music and dance, dramatic power is developmental. The capacity for mimicry, interpretation and creative dramatics develops in the child according to the experiences supplied by the school and the skills he masters in his general physical, intellectual and socio-emotional development. Contrary to much of the literature in the area of dramatics, the development of each of these forms is not a sequential process. Each may be developed independently, through the high school and college years, to promote skill and creativity. Though each form plays its most prominent role in the life of the child during his maturation process, each can be developed throughout his life.

From the beginning of life, every human being enjoys "play-acting" and imitating life around him. Through mimicking life in his early years, a child learns to behave like those around him. The joy of imitation is often squelched in children at an early age so it seeks its legitimate outlet in role-playing throughout life. Children play roles in their games, and mock their peers at play. Later, when this is frowned on, the growing child mimics in his games, and school plays and often affects the manners of the people he likes. High school and college students give vent to this creative drive by joining dramatic clubs where they can pretend they are someone else. Often these roles provide therapy in permitting them to become someone they would like to be. Our choice of a profession or a vocation is often determined by our ability to identify with an appealing role we see others playing.

We play dramatic roles every minute of every day and the roles change considerably from minute to minute. A young college female may play the role of a campus coed from 8 A.M. until 9 A.M. She changes her costume, her behavior and even her mode of speaking at 9 A.M. when she assumes the role of the student teacher. At 4 P.M., with school over, she returns to campus to play again the role of the student; doing her homework for the following day. At seven o'clock she plays the role of the leader as she acts as chairman of a sorority committee making plans for Spring Weekend; at eight o'clock her young man comes to call and she plays the role of a sweetheart. During the weekend she acts differently when going to church than when attending a basketball game. She also behaves differently as student council president than she does as big sister when she returns to her family to visit. "All the world's a stage!"

Many terms are used to identify the use of dramatics in a child's life. A definition of each of these terms is necessary if the material in this volume is to be clearly understood.

Dramatic Play. This term is used when referring to the spontaneous play of children. Many theories have been advanced regarding its meanings and functions. Some educators believe it to be a recapitulation of the maturing experience of the species. Some interpret children's dramatic play as a rehearsal for their future roles. Therapists and psychologists see it as a channel for growth in individual and social areas. Others see it as a means of emotional outlet or a means by which the child works out his problems. All agree that playing out a situation is the most natural way a child learns to live in the world around him and that permitting a child to play freely in a setting of security and acceptance is a sound way to enable him to deal satisfactorily and healthfully with the problems he faces in life. It aids in his emotional development and his social adjustment, it is essential to normal growth, and through it the child develops an empathy for others.

A good kindergarten and primary grade program makes provision for dramatic play as a technique by which children learn. Proper conditions are set for its development by providing dolls, pounding games, homemaking corners, dollhouses, a costume box, soap and water, replicas of tools such as ironing boards and toy

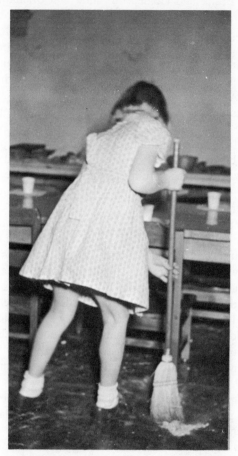

FIGURE 3–3. *Dramatic Play: Housekeeping*

trucks, and an out-of-doors play area. A part of the school day in all primary grades should be set aside for free dramatic play.

Proper psychological conditions are set by creating a permissive and accepting atmosphere where children feel free to imitate situations. The teacher should keep order, set limits and help the children wherever she can, but she should remain in the background as an observer most of the time. If she is sensitive during this time, she may learn more about the children and their problems than at any other part of the day.

Hartley, Frank and Goldenson[2] state that dramatic play serves many functions. Through this activity the child is given the opportunity (1) to imitate adults, (2) to play out real life roles in an intense way, (3) to reflect relationships and experiences, (4) to express pressing needs, (5) to release unacceptable impulses, (6) to reverse roles usually taken, (7) to mirror growth, and (8) to work out problems and experiment with solutions.

From this description of dramatic play, we can conclude that it is one of the most natural means of creative expression which a young child has. In fact, dramatic play is positive proof that all children are born creative. No one "teaches" a child how to dramatically play these roles—from the age of two or three he just does it. Dramatic play is a natural way for children to develop their creative powers.

In many schools dramatic play is not provided for in the curriculum above the kindergarten or first grade. The common belief, that as children mature "baby stuff" should be put away, is unfortunate. Dramatic play goes on in life and should be a part of the entire school program. A group of ten-year-old boys will play cops and robbers, Robin Hood or king of the castle just as ardently at the age of eleven as they played milkman at the age of four.

Dramatic play may be legitimately sustained in the elementary school program through its use as role playing. Ways to utilize this natural creative power are described in Chapter VI and in Book V of this series.[3]

Free Play. This term generally means the same as dramatic play. School programs allow children time for free play which they often use to engage in dramatic play.

Role-playing. This term has two general meanings. First it means the acting out by the young child of the sex role he will play in life. Studies in the play of children indicate that even at the nursery school age there are sex differences in the play of three and four-year-olds as children identify with the adults in their society. Girls tend to be mothers: they cook food, iron, play with dolls, clean the house, have tea parties and dress up. Boys play they are fathers, boat captains, baseball stars, garage men. This role identification helps the

[2] Ruth E. Hartley, Laurence K. Frank and Robert M. Goldenson, *Understanding Children's Play* (New York: Columbia University Press, 1952), pp. 27–28.

[3] James A. Smith, *Creative Teaching of the Social Studies in the Elementary School* (Boston: Allyn and Bacon, Inc., 1965), Chapt. IX.

child to play his proper role in society. But if children are too restricted, i.e., if boys are not allowed to play with dolls and girls are not allowed to be boat captains, less understanding of the opposite sex is developed and some of the ability to empathize is lost. Allowing children to engage in divergent roles in their play helps to develop their creativity. Creative boys tend to be more feminine than others because they enjoy some of the activities of the girls and vice versa. They are more open to life's experiences and can draw from them in order to create.

Another interpretation of role-playing is its deliberate use as a technique to help children solve their own socio-emotional problems. By acting out a problem which arises on the playground children come to see the problem in its entirety and can better arrive at a creative solution to it. Often, to develop empathy further, the role-reversal technique is used. In this situation the child who is accused of stealing a pen, for example, plays the role of the accuser, and the accuser plays the role of the accused. Children develop feelings of compassion and understanding for each other and problems are solved on a more intellectual and less emotional level.

Chapter IX of Book V gives many excellent illustrations of the use of role-playing and role-reversal as a part of a good social studies program.

Play therapy. Because dramatic play is a natural part of the child's growth pattern, it is used by psychologists and psychiatrists to identify the cause of disturbances in a child with problems. The child is placed in an environment with objects or symbols of objects of his everyday environment and allowed to do almost anything he wants to do. Limits are very broad and the skilled psychologist can get to the root of the child's problem after a series of sessions by observing the behavior of the child and recording his speech during the sessions.

Although play therapy is a technique used by highly trained specialists, there are implications for its use in the regular classroom. Often hostility and aggression can be worked out through play rather than through the infliction of harm on another person. Therapy provides a creative and positive outlet for the emotions. A good classroom will contain pounding boards, clay which may be pounded, dolls and puppets, shop benches with hammers and saws, toys such as pound-a-pegs, and time in the program when children can play out negative emotions and free themselves to concentrate on more positive things. Most of the creative arts: painting, composing music, writing poetry, dancing, acting and role-playing, can provide such emotional release. Thus negative feelings may be transposed into constructive, creative outlets.[4]

Dramatics or dramatization. This term applies to the acting out of a play, usually written as a script and read or recited. Dramatics can be an excellent tool for the development of creativity especially when the script is written by the children. Dramatics may take many forms, all of which are described in some detail in Book II:[5] puppet shows, shadow plays, pantomine, radio and television plays, choral speaking, book reports, etc. Dramatizations are generally planned to present before an audience. They may be impromptu or they may be a highly polished performance with scenery and costumes.

Examples of the way each of these types of dramatization may be used to develop creativity will be found in Chapter VI.

Summary

Throughout the ages, music, dance and drama have provided man with a creative means of communication and a positive outlet for his feelings. The chants and rhythms of the ancient tribes, the sign language of the American Indian, the ballads of the minstrels, the wagon plays of the medieval church—all were creative forms of teaching long before the average man became literate.

Since literacy has spread among the masses of people, knowledge and skill has developed and has been recorded in the areas of music, dance and drama, and each of these areas of primitive communication has risen to the status of an art in itself. As an art, each has been relegated to a place of honor in the elementary school curriculum where the science and skill of each is taught as part of the general education of all citizens.

Recent studies and writings in the area of creativity indicate that the creative development of each child would be greatly enhanced if, in addition to the teaching of the knowledge and skill necessary for literacy in each of these areas, they were restored in the school

[4] Virginia Mae Axline, *Play Therapy* (New York: Houghton Mifflin Company, 1947).

[5] James A. Smith, *Creative Teaching of the Language Arts in the Elementary School* (Boston: Allyn and Bacon, Inc., 1966).

curriculum to a place comparable to their place in the history of mankind: that of providing each child with a creative means of communication and a creative outlet for his emotional reactions to his environment.

TO THE COLLEGE STUDENT

1. Plan a way to present the Indian tune you created (as suggested on page 49) through a choral poem. Then try to put it to music by using a marimba or tuned glasses. Think of ways you can record this tune so a primary child who has no skill at reading music could play it.

2. Play some recordings of music and songs made in other lands. Include the folksongs of Japan, the veldt songs of Africa and the folksongs of America. Then decide what this music tells you. Can music rightfully be called an "international language"?

3. Discuss the value of dance recitals, such as those given by dancing schools, for primary children.

4. Trace the origin of the frug, the swim, the watusi, the waltz, the congo, the Charleston, the rhumba, the cakewalk and the foxtrot. Can you think of ways to teach these "patterned" established dances creatively?

5. There is a film which you will enjoy about techniques of dancing. It is called *Dancer's World* and is written by Martha Graham (30 min., color, Pennsylvania State University, University Park, Pennsylvania).

6. Another film you will enjoy which is centered around children is *Building Children's Personalities With Creative Dance* (29 min., b & w, U.C.L.A.).

TO THE CLASSROOM TEACHER

1. Encourage the children in your classroom to give one of their social studies reports by means of an interpretative dance rather than orally.

2. In one second grade classroom the teacher played lumberjack music and showed the children how to chop to the rhythm of the music. In another second grade classroom, the teacher played lumberjack music and asked each child to show her a movement which might be observed in a lumber camp. Which teacher is developing the principles of creative teaching?

3. In teaching social studies units, do you incorporate the dances of different cultures among your activities? How, for example, does the Virginia Reel reflect the life of the early settlers, and the Mexican hat dance reflect the life of that country, etc.? Of what social and emotional value are these dances to your children?

4. Think of all the ways your children play different roles during the day. How can you utilize this natural ability in developing social skills in your curriculum? (Example: dramatizing telephone conversations to develop telephone courtesies).

5. Music can be used effectively to generate imagery which can be used as a basis for creative painting, drawing or creative bodily interpretations. Select a jazz record, a classical record, a folk record and a popular record and note the different interpretations your children give to each.

TO THE COLLEGE STUDENT AND
THE CLASSROOM TEACHER

1. Simple instruments and devices may be used to help children create and record their original musical compositions. Some are: tuned glasses, a marimba, a simple xylophone, an autoharp and tuned spikes. Can you list others? Think of all the ways you can to help primary children record the tunes they create on these instruments so they will not forget them.

2. How would you go about developing a creative interpretative dance with intermediate grade children, using the following themes?

A football game.
The arrival of Santa Claus.
A visit to a machine shop.
A day at the races.
Building a skyscraper.

3. Think of all the ways you can integrate art, music and dramatic experiences into a single day's program in a classroom.

4. Note how you can see your own characteristics reflected in the children you teach. Observe how many times during a school day you use mimicry as a teaching technique.

5. In Book V of this series, *Creative Teaching of the Social Studies in the Elementary School,* dramatics and role-playing are described as ways to solve social problems. How might rhythms or dance be used in a similar fashion?

6. In Book I, the skills and characteristics of creative children are listed. Examine your daily program and observe ways you are already developing these skills (Example: developing visual acuity in reading).

7. A film you will enjoy is *Dance Demonstration* (10 min., color, Perry Mansfield).

SELECTED BIBLIOGRAPHY

ANDREWS, GLADYS. *Creative Rhythmic Movement for Children.* Englewood Cliffs: Prentice-Hall, Inc., 1954.

ANDREWS, GLADYS, JEANETTE SAURBORN and ELSA SCHNEIDER. *Physical Education for Boys and Girls.* Boston: Allyn and Bacon, Inc., 1960.

AXLINE, VIRGINIA M. *Play Therapy.* New York: Houghton Mifflin Co., 1947.

ELLISON, ALFRED. *Music With Children.* New York: McGraw-Hill Book Co., 1959.

HARTLEY, RUTH E., LAURENCE K. FRANK and ROBERT GOLDENSON. *Understanding Children's Play,* New York: Columbia University Press, 1952.

LEONARD, CHARLES and ROBERT W. HOUSE. *Foundations and Principles of Music Education.* New York: McGraw-Hill Book Co., 1959.

MURRAY, RUTH LOVELL. *Dance in Elementary Education.* New York: Harper & Row, Publishers, Inc., 1963.

SIKS, GERALDINE B. *Creative Dramatics: An Art for Children.* New York: Harper & Row, Publishers, Inc., 1958.

SLIND, LLOYD H. and EVAN D. DAVIS. *Bringing Music to Children.* New York: Harper & Row, Publishers, Inc., 1964.

STEIN, MORRIS and SHIRLEY J. HEINZE. *Creativity and the Individual.* Glencoe: Free Press of Glencoe, Inc., 1960.

STRANG, R. M. "Creativity in the Elementary Classroom," *National Edu-* ed. Harold H. Anderson. New York: Harper & Row, Publishers, Inc., 1959, 182.

STODDARD, G., "Creativity in Education," *Creativity and Its' Cultivation, cation Association Journal,* L (March 1961), 20–22.

TAYLOR, CALVIN (ed.), *Widening Horizons in Creativity* (Proceedings of the Fifth Utah Creativity Research Conference), 1964.

TORRANCE, E. PAUL (ed.), *Creativity.* Minneapolis: University of Minnesota, Center for Continuation Study of the General Extension Division, 1959.

————. *Guiding Creative Talent.* Englewood Cliffs: Prentice Hall, Inc., 1963.

————. *Rewarding Creative Behavior.* Englewood Cliffs: Prentice Hall, Inc., 1965.

Part Two

The Nurture of Creativity Through the Creative Arts

An Overview

Creativity cannot be taught as a subject or skill. If the development of creativity in children is to be an objective of the elementary school, caution must be exercised so that all areas of the curriculum contribute to its growth. In Part Two of this volume, I have selected material which may be used to develop creativity in children through the application of the creative principles stated in Chapter I and the knowledge of children and their relation to the creative arts stated in Chapter II. I have been guided in my selection by the following criteria:

1. *Novelty.* I feel that new ideas stimulate children so I have selected materials which will provide children with new experiences, affording them the opportunity to learn new skills and to apply them in divergent ways to produce creative products.

2. *Principles.* Each illustration or suggestion, if properly used within the framework of the teaching principles presented in Chapters I and II, will develop the powers of creativity and will set conditions for creative teaching. If improperly used, however, many of the illustrations on the following pages can defeat the goal of developing creative power. The variable in each instance is the teacher; her method must follow the principles stated in Chapter I or creativity will not be nurtured.

3. *Functionalism.* A first rule of all art expression is that it must be functional, that is, it must serve the purpose for which it was made. A beautiful office building loses much of its beauty if it is so poorly designed inside that the offices are too small, improperly equipped or poorly organized. The materials on the following pages were selected because they may be integrated with the total school program to make learning more functional or they may be used for art's sake to make art more enjoyable, or for the children's sake to make life more beautiful and livable.

4. *Generality.* I chose the following illustrations because they are general enough to be presented in many ways and to be adapted to many age levels.

Creative Teaching Through Art

IV

Child art has a character of its own. Spontaneous self-expression through means of art materials is natural and fundamentally satisfying to all children. Children cannot approach art activities in the same way that adults do and should never have adult forms imposed on them ... The real test of whether a child's art is "good" is not how much the tree he has drawn represents the natural appearance of the tree, but how fully the child, when working, has entered into a personal reaction of his own to the tree and its environment . . .[1]

ELLSWORTH AND ANDREWS

TO THE READER

After you read this chapter, experiment with some of the media mentioned here with which you have not had experience before. Do you go through the same stages in art development that children do?

Introduction

The creative teaching of art can contribute to the growth of creative power in many ways: (1) It contributes through the obvious; children will create with the materials at hand rendering either the process or the product creative. (2) It presents a challenge to creative thinking and creative problem solving by the manner in which it is presented. A teacher may present a group of children with a cart full of art materials of all kinds or with a piece of white paper and some black paint and pose the problem: "Using any of these materials, construct an art product which shows *fear*." In the second situation, the child is restricted in his materials and his mind cannot take flight as it can in the first situation, but both situations are highly tension-producing. In the second situation, the child must be *more* creative than in the first. (3) It provides an opportunity for open-ended learning situations where skills may be used in divergent ways.

[1] Maud Ellsworth and Michael Andrews, *Growing with Art: A Teacher's Book*. (Syracuse: The L. W. Singer Co.) Centerpieces, p. 1.

(4) It develops those characteristics and traits mentioned in Chapters I and II which are essential for creative development. (5) It contributes to personal fulfillment and adds to the self-realization of the individual. (6) It provides the child with experiences parallel to his development. (7) It provides a manner by which individual differences can be developed in a group process and consequently promotes the growth of the whole child. (8) It provides a way to develop skills which may be used to enrich the total school curriculum so the total school curriculum becomes a source of developing creative power.

Proper conditions, as outlined in Chapter II, are necessary for the art period. A strong tension-building motivation is necessary and all judgment, except the suggestions of the teacher are deferred. Almost any media may be used and almost any subject matter area or school situation may provide the stimulus for an art production. Following are some general suggestions for correlation with the rest of the school day. Most of the techniques suggested are known to classroom teachers and art teachers. Each should be introduced as a technique for solving some particular problem which may be expressed through an art media. Problems are implied through examples in parenthesis after some of the items on the list.

Creative thinking and forms of thinking related to creative thinking are developed through the proper use of these activities. As an example, illustrating stories and poems calls for elaboration and interpretation on the part of the child. He must use his imagination to fill in the gaps in knowledge given by the poem or story. In making murals, for example, children must make predictions on the basis of knowledge given.

Each activity listed calls for the development of empathy, a quality necessary to sound human relations and basic art expression. Many of these techniques motivate self-learning in that they encourage more extensive reading and a search for additional knowledge. Material must be synthesized and concepts developed before ideas can be expressed in a single art form or a combination of art forms. Convergent thought processes are developed by learning the technique and divergent thinking processes are developed when the technique is used to solve a problem.

Common Experiences Used to Develop Creative Art Expression

1. Illustrate stories and poems. (What is the author saying to you? How does he make *you* feel?)
2. Make get-well cards. (What can we do to let mother know we love her? to make Joe happier while he is in the hospital?)
3. Make murals for social studies and literature projects.
4. Make clay objects. (How did the earth look in prehistoric times? What are some useful gifts for father on Father's Day?)
5. Try sawdust and papier-mâché modeling. (Let's make imaginary animals for our make-believe zoo.)
6. Make stick, finger, fist or paper bag puppets. (How can we show other ways to solve this playground problem?)
7. Build doll houses, forts or models. (Show the class how an adobe hut is made).
8. Make dioramas for literature and social studies.
9. Make stuffed toys. (What kinds of animals can we make for our indoor circus?)
10. Design holiday decorations.
11. Illustrate original stories and books.
12. Make masks from paper plates, papier-mâché, aluminum foil and paper bags. (Represent your favorite character in our Book Week Program.)
13. Make gifts.
14. Try soap sculpture.
15. Try crayon work.
16. Use tempera and powder paint.
17. Use cut paper designs.
18. Make torn paper designs.
19. Make cloth designs. (Make charts using real swatches of fabrics to show how each is used.)
20. Make montages. (How can we show *happiness* with these materials?)
21. Make scrap wood designs.
22. Try "junk" montages.
23. Try papier-mâché moulding.
24. Draw portraits. (How can we show mother and father where you sit at our school Open House?)
25. Draw pictures of "My Family" and "My Friends."
26. Paint scenery for plays.
27. Make puppet shows, costumes and scenery.
28. Design Easter hats.
29. Paint abstractions such as "Happiness," "Sadness," etc.
30. Make valentines.
31. Make ornaments for the Christmas tree from odds and ends.

32. Make mobiles. (Let's show everyone all the stories by Dr. Suess that we have read.)
33. Make posters.
34. Try fingerpainting.
35. Design maps. (How do we get to school by walking? If we take a bus?)
36. Construct wire modelings.
37. Try crayon etching.
38. Do stencil work.
39. Make chalk drawings.
40. Make wet chalk drawings.
41. Make sponge and stick paintings.
42. Make spatter painting.
43. Make potato prints.
44. Make stick prints.
45. Make block prints. (How can we design a cover for many programs for our play?)
46. Make a box water color painting.
47. Make a curled paper construction.
48. Make yarn drawings.
49. Try sewing yarn on burlap.
50. Try wood construction.
51. Make signs.
52. Draw cartoons. (Let's create our own comic character for our school newspaper.)
53. Try pipe cleaner sculpture.

INTERMEDIATE GRADES

To the above list add such activities as:

1. Felt pen drawing and lettering. (How can we show everyone where our room centers are? Who will make charts for our questions for our unit so we can see them anywhere in the room?)
2. Tile making and designing.
3. Building forms over crushed paper. (How can we show the terrain of the New England States?)
4. Relief maps.
5. Plaster of Paris moulding.
6. Wooden or paper carton models of types of communication, historical events, scientific inventions, etc.
7. Dioramas showing historical events or natural resources.
8. Gifts. (What kinds of gifts can we make that we can package and send to our school in Holland?)
9. Jewelry making.
10. Construction of kites.
11. Book making.
12. Charcoal drawing.
13. Pencil drawing.

14. Photographic compositions.
15. Three-dimensional posters and bulletin boards.
16. Tissue paper art work. (What is another way to create the effect of stained glass windows?)
17. Table top mock-ups of social studies projects.
18. Costumes. (What kind of clothing did Robin Hood and King Richard wear?)
19. Maps and globes.
20. Wax carving.
21. Models: igloos, wigwams, etc.
22. Pottery making.
23. Weaving.
24. Sewing patchwork quilts, etc.
25. Sculptoring.
26. Charts.
27. Appliqué work.
28. Blockprint on fabrics.
29. Textile painting.
30. Tie-dying. (What is a quick method we can use to make colorful curtains for our windows?)
31. Batik work.
32. Flannel board paintings. (Show anger with these colored pieces of flannel on the flannel board.)
33. Cake and cupcake decorating for parties.
34. Popcorn balls for parties, pressed into various shapes and decorated.
35. Cartoon strips.
36. Make advertisements, slogans, etc. to publicize school events.
37. Design and print Christmas cards.

The following activities are suggested for the purpose of setting conditions for creative art activities by keeping certain materials available in the classroom with which children may experiment and explore.

1. Keep a box of scrap materials (buttons, sticks, shells, sponges, straw, rope, paper lace, etc.) to be dipped in paint and placed on paper to make all-over designs.

2. Use photographs or pictures from magazines and newspapers to make a montage.

3. Make a bas-relief by filling a metal jar lid with plasticene and covering the entire lid with metal foil. Blunt tools may then be used to push a design into the foil.

4. Glue seeds, grain and other dried materials on a piece of cardboard to make a mosaic.

5. Arrange many various textured articles on a sheet of paper (a piece of screen, some burlap, some rubber bands, paper clips,

string, yarn, etc.). Place another sheet of paper over the arranged shape. Using a brayer and blockprint ink, make a rubbing. A soft crayon will also work.

6. Dip linoleum brayers into various colored paints and roll out on large sheets of paper to make all-over designs.

7. Make crayon drawings on tissue paper. Press with a hot iron.

8. Dampen paper with turpentine. Make a design with crayons.

9. Use combs, pieces of cardboard, large bolts, screws, etc. for texture effects when finger painting.

10. Add other materials, such as shells, sand, sequins, glitter, etc., to the design when finger painting. Allow them to dry in the painting.

11. Try fingerpainting on slippery surfaces such as aluminum foil, oilcloth and old photographic plates.

12. Mix sawdust and asbestos powder with wallpaper paste for modeling.

13. Model with salt and flour dough.

14. Cut rubber shapes from an inner tube or a sheet of cork. Glue them on a rolling pin. Ink and use for an all-over design by rolling it over book covers, etc.

15. Use soft bricks for bas-relief carving.

16. Make wire figures, painted or dipped in melted wax.

17. Paint with tools other than a brush (a piece of frayed rope, cotton swabs, sponges, crumpled paper, toothbrushes) or make your own brush.

18. Take a sheet of paper: Crumple it, flatten it out, then paint on it.

19. Have each child draw two circles on a large piece of paper and then exchange them with his neighbor. The children are to use their imaginations and see what they can make using the two circles.

Art Appreciation Activities to Stimulate Creative Thinking

1. Take "looking walks" to find beauty in line, form, color, texture and pattern.

2. Make flower arrangements in classroom; keep a beauty center.

3. Make flower arrangements for party tables.

4. Enjoy famous paintings.

5. Have a "touching table" where children can enjoy the feel of

articles: velvet, ribbon, soft toys, sandpaper, glass, worn stones, marbles, etc.

6. Arrange bulletin boards and exhibits.

7. Arrange and decorate a library corner in the classroom.

8. Select, mount and hang the childrens' own paintings.

9. Discuss and evaluate the childrens' paintings and other art work.

10. Take trips to museums and local art exhibits.

Contrived Experiences to Develop Creativity Through Art

The following experiences have been selected because they are unusual. They have been tried with children of all ages with some very satisfying results. Teachers are encouraged to use them, but also to keep expanding their own creativity by thinking of related or new ideas to try with their own students.

Make an art film. Buy 25 feet of white "leader" film from a photographer. (Leader film is the white film put on the beginning of each film to thread it through the projector. It is translucent but not transparent and it will take certain kinds of water paint, India ink and felt pen ink. The color applied will project on a screen.) Spread the film out around the table and encourage each child to decorate about a foot of it in any way he wants to. Tell him it is to be put through the film projector but to do what he wishes with his section of the film.

When it is finished put the film through the projector on silent speed and the children will see their designs dance and flit before them in a variety of movements.

After the film has been shown, play several records and have children select the record which best goes with the film. Then play both the film and the record together.

Mr. Barton's fifth grade made such a film. The designs were short, choppy, and staccato. To accompany them the children chose a honky-tonk piano record. After the music and the record had been played together, Mr. Barton played the record independently and asked the children to write to the music. He then put the music on a tape, along with what the children had written. First he played a little of the music, then he passed the microphone to the first child who read what he had written as Mr. Barton lowered the volume on the record. While the mike was being passed to the next child, Mr. Barton raised the volume. As soon as he lowered it, the second child read into the mike. After the whole group had read, the sound track was played while the film was shown. The feeling of the film was then expressed in several ways: through moving color, through music and through the original poetry and prose of the children.

Miss Ayres, in the kindergarten, tried the same technique with her class. The kindergarteners used long, bold strokes on the film as kindergarten children often do. When Miss Ayres played the records, the children chose "The Blue Danube Waltz" to accompany their film. Miss Ayres also allowed the children to record their voices on the tape with a musical background. The product she obtained was extremely different from that obtained by Mr. Barton.

Go on a sketching trip. Take a walk around the school with sketching pad or clipboard and paper. Also take crayons, colored chalk or a water paint set. Find a scene or group of interesting forms (a cluster of housetops, a grouping of playground equipment) and go to work! The trip may be prefaced by some discussion which will stimulate children to express in many ways the scene they paint.

Cut paper mobiles. Mobiles may be created in many ways by the use of cut paper to make a unit in literature or social studies more interesting (see Books II and V).[2] Designs and shapes can be cut in various patterns and fitted, stapled or glued together. These can be suspended from bare branches sprayed with tempera paint or from sticks or wires suspended from the ceiling in various patterns.

To vary the procedure and add depth to the creative process, the teacher may someday give the children strips of assorted paper and a stapler. By bending, twisting and folding the strips, flat abstract designs of birds, fish, people and other objects will result in a different type of mobile.

Miss Davis's third grade class had constructed many interesting mobiles. To challenge their creative abilities, Miss Davis showed the children how to cut a large sheet of paper so that it would open to form a three-dimensional globe. She taught them the basic principle that two-dimensional paper, when folded, could be made three-dimensional if cuts were made in the paper *up to* a fold but not *through* it. After the children, working in groups, had made the globes (all varying somewhat in form), Miss Davis introduced a box of miscellaneous materials and challenged the children to decorate the globes so that each was as different as possible from any other.

It was spring and many interesting globes, decorated by spring

[2] James A. Smith, *Creative Teaching of the Language Arts in the Elementary School.* Boston: Allyn and Bacon, 1967; and *Creative Teaching of the Social Studies in the Elementary School.* Boston: Allyn and Bacon, 1967.

symbols, resulted. Some children suspended artificial flowers in the little openings in the cut paper. Others put cotton rabbits or May flowers inside the globes. These mobiles, suspended from the ceiling by threads, made beautiful classroom decorations.

Mrs. Elson, the first grade teacher, borrowed Miss Davis's idea but had the children make a mobile about each of the community helpers which the class was studying in social studies. In the center of one globe the children suspended a cardboard policeman. In each of the small openings on the outer surface of the globe they hung the symbols which they associated with the policeman such as his badge, his stick, his cap, and various traffic signals.

Mr. Ebberhart, a Junior High School teacher, also borrowed Miss Davis's idea and had his seventh graders adorn the mobiles with garden themes to decorate the gymnasium for the spring dance.

The problem of making one material or one shape work many ways can be a very creative challenge to children of all ages.

Make Stabiles. Using plaster of Paris as a base, let children make design stabiles with straws, colored shapes of oaktag, string, thread holders, beautiful junk, etc.

Children enjoy being able to select various pieces for their stabile.

Varying of One Form. Other challenging situations can be created by giving the children similar shapes and assigning them the job of making the insides as different as possible. Some examples follow.

Sparkle Wreaths. Give the children a jar rubber such as those used for home canning purposes. Provide a box of small pins, ribbon, sequins, sparkle, colored pipe cleaners, etc. and ask them to make a lapel wreath for their mothers for Christmas. Each one is to be as different as possible from all others.

Wreaths. A paper plate or a coat hanger bent in oval form can be the original form from which the children construct their individual wreaths. They may use plastic bags, tissue paper, crepe paper, evergreen, glitter, Christmas tree balls, pine cones, fruit, candy, gourds, cellophane, holly, buttons, cloth, etc.

Spinning tops. Old records can be painted with tempera paint and then used as a spinning top. A small screw pushed through the center hole provides the point needed. The child then has a new form to fill—a circular one. The spinning does interesting things to the colored designs.

Designs can also be created by using scrap paper of various shapes and asking children to fill in a design to fit the outer shape of the paper. All media may be used to do this.

Making Christmas tree ornaments. Children can make their own Christmas tree ornaments in a variety of ways. Almost all materials can be used but unusual ones can be created from unusual materials. Some materials which lend themselves to this are ice cream cones (which can be glued, sprayed and painted in many ways), tin can covers (which can be snipped, cut or bent into many shapes), styrofoam balls (which can be painted or stuck full of interesting objects), colored art tissue or cellophane (which can be crumpled or folded) and paper cups (which can be glued, colored and decorated in many varying shapes).

Making Enamel Abstracts. Interesting free designs may be created from enamel or wood. Ask the children to bring from home old, flat pieces of plywood or wood with an interesting grain and left-over cans of enamel paint. Square the piece of wood and tape a border on it with masking tape. Using a wide brush, paint over the exposed part of the wood within the border with white, flat paint. While the paint is still wet, drip, brush or daub the colored enamels on it. (They can be thinned with turpentine so they run easily.) Tilting the board will help to mix the colors or run them together for interesting effects. When the desired design has been obtained, allow the paints to dry. Then peel off the masking tape, exposing a wooden border. Shellac over the entire painting to preserve it and to highlight the grain in the wood.

Making Corrugated Cardboard Designs. New, challenging media can often be found in interesting places. Cardboard cartons, for example, add a new dimension to children's combined efforts in cutting and painting. Have the children draw a design on a piece of corrugated cardboard and with a letter opener or some other blunt instrument, cut along the design. Then parts of the design may be peeled away to expose the corrugated cardboard beneath. Paint and other materials may be added to give an interesting bas-relief effect.

Seeing Shape Relationships. It is always interesting to see how children can build new concepts in shape relationships. Materials of interesting shapes can be brought from home or collected over a period of time, and then spread out on a big table before the children with the challenge to choose any of the articles, to combine them, paint them, or add to them to create something new and practical.

Jimmy took two old funnels and made his mother a beautiful candle holder (Figure 4–1).

FIGURE 4–1. *Jimmy's candle holder*

Bill used funnels and flower pots to make hanging lamps for his room (FIGURE 4–2).

Tin Foil Mask Crafting. Blow up a balloon, then wrap two or three layers of tin foil around it. After breaking the balloon, the tin foil can be shaped to suit the child and decorated with sequins, colored toothpicks, etc. also.

Tin foil wrapped around beach balls will make large enough masks to be set on the shoulders of children. The beach balls can be deflated, leaving the mask hollow. This is excellent for making animal heads for plays or use in making other costumes.

Making Stuffed Animals. Paper bags stuffed with shreds of paper can make effective animals or figures. Fold over the ends of the bag and glue them together. Use a small one for the head, a large one for the body and use mailing tubes as legs. Fasten the animal together with pins or thread and paint it with tempera (FIGURE 4–3).

Printing Processes. Often little children want to make several get well or Christmas cards to give to friends, but do not want to

FIGURE 4–2. *Bill's lamps*

draw each one individually. Or perhaps they would like to make programs for a play and they want them to be alike. This is a good opportunity to introduce them to a simple form of printing quite comparable to the silk screen process. (This process is good only for silhouettes.)

Place a piece of organdy, drawn upon with a crayon, between two embroidery hoops. The drawing must be done heavily and with wax crayon so as to make certain that it is thick. Place the hoops flat on the paper on which the design is to be printed. With a rubber spatula, rub finger paint or thick tempera paint over the organdy. The paint will penetrate the organdy and go through to the paper, but will not penetrate the wax design. This stencil may be used many times.

Printing with Blotters. Soft blotters may be used in a similar fashion to organdy. Crayon (with wax crayons) a design on a soft blotter. Brush it with a brush full of thick tempera or finger paint, then blot the design on the paper. Do not get the blotter too wet or the paint too thick. The job will be easier if the blotter is glued (with water-resisting glue) on a block of wood.

FIGURE 4–3. *Stuffed paper animals provide a new media for expression.*

Printing with innertubes, sponges and vegetables. Designs may easily be cut from old innertubes, sponges or into vegetables and printed as above.

For young children a stamping pad provides a quick and easy way to print. This can be easily made by folding some paper towels into an even square and soaking them with water. Ring out the excess water and place the folded towels on a saucer. Soak them with paint and allow a few minutes for the paint to be absorbed by the towels. Now they will serve as a usable stamp pad.

Making Candles. There are many ways children can make candles and work with a new media: *wax*. Caution must be exercised so that children do not work with the hot wax. The teacher should do any pouring of the hot wax and allow the children to have the experience of working with the cold wax, making unusual shapes out of the candle.

Ask the children to bring old candle stubs, paraffin or old wax objects to school. When a large supply has been collected, the teacher can melt them down. Very clever candles can be made by cutting blocks of paraffin into smaller blocks, heating one side of the paraffin and slapping two of the blocks together with a string wick between them. This provides a quick, easy candle to decorate. Thick candles can be made simply by heating blocks of paraffin and sticking them together. White candles and paraffin will, of course, make white wax.

Red wax can be obtained by melting down white wax or pink wax and adding all the small pieces of left-over red crayons, while green candles can be made by melting together any old pieces of blue, green or yellow wax or by adding green left-over crayon butts.

When the wax is melted the teacher can pour it into moulds. Short, squatty candles may be obtained by using waxed, half-pint milk cartons as a mould. Quart milk cartons make bigger candles. Round candles can be made by filling two round tea cups and allowing them to set. After they have set, remove the two hemispheres from the cups, warm the top side of one, lay a string on it for a wick and stick it to the other one.

Candles may be decorated in many ways. They may be carved with blunt instruments, or painted with tempera paints (if a little soap powder is first added to the paint). They may also be covered with "candle snow" which is made by melting some paraffin in a pan and then whipping it with an egg beater. While the frothy paraffin is still warm, flick it onto the candle with a fork. When it cools it will harden and sequins, glitter, shells and other decorations may be added to make the candles gay and suitable for any occasion.

Candles may also be made by dipping and then decorating the dipped candles.

Making Constructions. The teacher makes available interesting, discarded materials: foil paper, beads, feathers, buttons, wood scraps, braid, lace, soft wire, bright wrapping paper scraps, etc. plus a stapler, paste and rubber and airplane cement. Some possibilities of using the materials and adhesives should be discussed by the group, but the charm of the finished product and the joy of creating depends upon the pupil being free to explore and experiment, using his own, problem-solving ingenuity.

In making wire constructions any kind of "friendly" wire (expressive word meaning easily manipulated, used by a sixth grade boy) may be used. The construction is up to the child; he winds and twists abstractions or realistic figures. A wood base, prepared by the child, gives him added experience in measuring, sawing and finishing.

Making Masks. Make masks, using a variety of materials and techniques:

1. Folded colored construction paper.
2. Papier-mâché put over a clay mould.
3. Papier-mâché built up over either a mould of wadded paper, or a box.
4. Decorated packing boxes.
5. Several crushed layers of tin foil over a beach ball, with cut out eyes, nose and mouth, decorated with materials. It will set over the child's head.
6. Large paper bags.
7. Crepe paper crushed over various shapes.
8. Paper plates.

Glass Art. Broken pieces of colored glass salvaged from the glass factory, from broken bottles or from dishes at home provide materials for challenging art experiences. They may be arranged in beautiful designs by pushing them gently into wet sand confined within a box cover, and saved by pouring plaster of Paris on the design when it is complete. When the plaster sets, break the box cover, brush off the dried sand with a soft brush and the glass mosaic can be framed and used as a wall plaque or for other decorative purposes. Care must be taken to instruct the children in how to work carefully with the glass.

Flat pieces of glass may be glued to table tops, or to pieces of wood with Elmer's Glue—then brushed over with grout to make coffee table tops or hot plate tiles.

Children may collect cheap or old glasses from home or from

the five and ten cent store. They may be made into a Christmas hurricane candle by placing a wick in the middle and filling it with melted wax. Glitter, sequins, tiny angels, sprigs of holly, Christmas tinsel and Christmas bows can be glued to the outside of the glass.

Adhesive tape may be cut in circles and used to hold colored pieces of glass onto strings. Suspended from wires or used to fill wire shapes, these make beautiful mobiles, especially when they are hung in a window where the sunlight may play on them, or under an artificial or colored light.

If children can find two glasses exactly alike, they may create beautiful designs by filling them with various materials and then tipping one glass upside down over another, fastening them together with scotch tape and adding decorations to the outside. Beautiful Christmas ornaments can be made in this way with tinsel, colored balls, colored stars, cellophane, discarded ribbon and Christmas package decorations. Also tiny nativity scenes may be built in the glasses. (Beer glasses are especially good for this.)

Flat pieces of glass may be used to make slides to go with a favorite piece of literature or to illustrate the children's poems (see page 84 of this book).

Making String Designs. Beautiful string designs may be constructed by using the covers of boxes of various sizes or flat pieces of cardboard. Put nicks along the edges and stretch colored string from one side of the cardboard to the other, hooking it through the nicks. Another application of the same idea is to make large wooden frames with tacks along the edges for hooking on the string. These can be used as three-dimensional pictures or as room dividers.

Resist Process. Make a picture or design with wax crayon, leaving some background areas uncolored. Choose light, bright colors and apply them heavily so that no spots of paper show through the crayon. Paint over the entire paper with dark poster paint of medium consistency. Black, dark blue or dark violet usually give the best results. A variation in results may be obtained by using dark but bright crayons and painting them with white, yellow or other light colors.

String or Yarn Mesh Balloons. Blow up a balloon and tie it tightly. Cut several pieces of assorted string or yarn about one yard long. Dip the pieces into paste (such as wallpaper paste) or a thick cornstarch solution which may be colored by adding powdered paint. Wrap the strings around a balloon, pulling them between fingers lightly to remove excess paste. The string may be wrapped around the

FIGURE 4–4. *Glass ornaments.* (*made from old Christmas decorations and cheap glasses*)

balloon or it may be applied in the form of a design. When the string is dry, untie the balloon and let the air out slowly. The hollow yarn ball that results can then be used for many purposes, and may provide the children with a new experience in problem solving.

In Miss Power's third grade the children made these balls at Christmas time. They glued sequins, glitter and tiny designs on the outside and dropped tiny bells, pine cones, and angels inside. They then used the balls as Christmas tree decorations.

At Easter time in Mr. Johnson's fifth grade, the children made yarn balls and decorated them with tiny spring flowers, sequins, and Easter seals. Inside they placed flower gardens or nests of eggs, cotton rabbits and chickens. They used their creations as centerpieces for the Easter table.

Mrs. Fanto, a second grade teacher, used them to make an

attractive abstract mobile by suspending the varicolored, decorated balls by strings from the branch of a tree hung from the ceiling.

Slides. Slides are easy to make and provide the children with an interesting media to explore. Kits for making slides may be purchased, but the slides can be made inexpensively with a few basic materials. Pieces of glass can be cut to the correct size with a glass cutter. Etching cream can be purchased by the tube and may be rubbed over the glass with the fingers to make it cloudy. After the excess cream is rinsed off, the children may draw on it directly with Keystone colored crayons which will project color on a screen. India ink or felt pens may also be used to project colors. Variations in slides may be used by placing colored pieces of cellophane between two pieces of glass and taping them together. Slides make an exciting means for telling stories and giving social studies reports.

Painting to Music. Creative expression can be fostered when children are alerted to the fact that moods can be expressed in many ways. Music of varying moods can be played while children paint. Any kind of paint will do but fingerpaint is especially appropriate for young children because it is less inhibiting than painting which involves brushes and other tools. Soap paint, tempera paint and crayons can be sprinkled with sand or glitter to create interesting effects.

Painting Words. In the intermediate grades, symbolism in painting (which is often lost at this level) can be developed by placing words (preferably those which children have recently discovered) on the chalk board and encouraging the children to paint them. Some good words for this are: joy, happiness, anger, fear, love, beauty, sadness, loneliness, etc. Sometimes phrases challenge the children to do interesting things. Some which might be used are:

> What color is loneliness?
> Paint the thunderstorm you hear.
> Paint the silence of snow.
> Paint the noise of the circus.

String Painting. Cut string of various thicknesses into different lengths. Fill shallow bowls with thick tempera paint or colored wallpaper paste and let the children dip the string in the colored media. They then make tracings on varicolored paper by arranging the string in various designs. Some children will want to leave the string on the paper where it will stick when the paint drys.

Sand Moulding. Sand moulding is similar to making glass

mosaics (see page 81 of this book). The children place wet sand in the top of an old box, or in any similar container. In the shallow layer of sand they poke and then remove objects which will make designs in the sand: shells, potato mashers, buttons, sticks, the bottom of fancy glasses, beads, marbles, chain links—almost anything may be used. The design can be preserved by mixing plaster of Paris to the consistency of tomato soup, pouring it gently over the design until it is about one-fourth inch thick, allowing the plaster of Paris to dry, then lifting it from the box. Any sand that clings to the mould should be allowed to dry and then brushed off with a soft brush. The moulds may be further decorated with paint and other media.

Some children will want to make a shape in the sand so that the mould will have an outline. In this way fish shapes, tree shapes or any other shape can give the finished mould greater interest and will present a new problem-solving situation for the child.

Sculpting. Sculpting, in a variety of forms, can be challenging to children.

Soft stone. Sandstone is a good media for this.

Plaster of Paris. Pour wet plaster into paper ice cream tubs or boxes of various sizes and shapes. When the plaster is dry, tear away the carton and use the remaining block for sculpting.

Snow. Snow sculpture always provides a new soft, pliable yet firm media. It can be moulded or sculpted or colored by spraying tempera or alabastine paint on it.

Flower Arrangements. Relationships between shapes and color can be developed by having the children arrange flowers. A beauty spot in the room will focus attention on a new arrangement for each day (see page 174). In the fall, milkweed pods, seed pods and various shapes of weeds and leaves can be collected, dried or pressed for winter use. A shallow shadowbox, cut from a large carton, can be hung in a conspicuous place to house such arrangements.

Scratch Drawings. Color a sheet of tag board or hard-surfaced paper with different bright, wax crayons. Apply the crayons heavily and thickly. After the entire sheet is covered, go over it again with black wax crayon. Then, using combs, nails, leather tools, blunt scissors and a variety of other tools, scratch designs in the black crayon. The colors underneath will show through and children will find the opportunity to use many creative ideas in this simple form of etching.

Tin Can Art. If caution is exercised so that children do not cut themselves, many creative experiences can result from the use of tin can covers, saved by the mothers and donated to the school. A simple precaution to take is to tell all children to hold the cover firmly in the middle, to decide where he is going with his cut, and then to go there with one direct cut. It is the hesitant cuts which may prick the child. Any sturdy scissors may be used to make the cut.

Tin can covers may be fastened together in various patterns. They may be twisted and embellished with beads, glitter, sequins, or small Christmas tree ornaments. They may be used in wreath decorations or in mobiles. They may be bent into tiny bells and hung on yarn. They may be painted and bent into various shapes or hung on strings so they shimmer in the changing light of the room. They may also be used for making lapel decorations or jewelry.

Staple Designs. Long strips of colored construction paper can be cut and used to make interesting designs by stapling them together in a variety of ways. Staple an uneven number of strips together at one end. Then by gathering the other strips up and stapling in various loops and folds to the center strip some interesting designs can be created. These designs can be arranged on blank walls in attractive designs, hung in windows or suspended on strings from the light fixtures. When made in miniature they are excellent Christmas tree ornaments.

Old Greeting Card Art. Collect old post cards and greeting cards and use the pretty, comical, sparkly or bright parts of them which are especially adaptable to build paper mosaics and montages. Magazine pictures and advertisements can also be effectively used in this manner. Some children will enjoy combining these cutouts with their paintings to create some currently popular "pop" art.

Frosting Art. Children can experience an entirely new texture if colored cake icing is placed in bowls on a table and a cake decorator set or two is used to decorate cupcakes, cakes or pies for a school party.

Plaster of Paris Art. One day, in a fifth grade classroom, children were making sand mosaics. Joey was mixing plaster of Paris to pour over the mosaics. After stirring the mixture to the consistency of heavy whipped cream, he said, "This would be good to decorate cakes with." Miss Fellows, his teacher, seized his idea and encouraged him to experiment with the cake decorator set which the class used many times. Joey put the mixture into a set and tried it out. This led to some grand and wonderful experiments with plaster of Paris. First the children decorated flat surfaces, then they discovered that they could add powdered paint to the mixture and have a variety of colored plaster of Paris. They ended with elaborate constructions made from wire and string (such as the wound string balloons mentioned above), which they covered with plaster of Paris and then decorated with the designs which emerge from the little caps on the cake decorator. The children learned that with this media they must work quickly and that they must wash off their cake decorators before the plaster hardened. Some very creative products resulted under these new conditions, where the pressure of time forced the children to think and act quickly.

Modeling. Cornstarch clay recipe: 4 tbsp. cornstarch, 8 tbsp. salt and 8 tbsp. boiling water.

Mix salt and cornstarch. Pour boiling water over mixture and stir until salt is dissolved. Heat and stir again until mixture forms soft ball in middle of pan. Remove and knead for 10 minutes. Wrap in wax paper and keep in tightly covered jar for preservation. Can be punched, rolled, squeezed, cut in shapes, and so on.

Whipped Soap Art. One cup of soap flakes can be dissolved in one cup of warm water. After another cup of hot water is added, the mixture is placed in an electric beater until it is frothy and thick. This mixture can be applied to various surfaces with a fork and then used as a base for holding decorative objects in place. The mixture may be colored with the addition of a little powdered paint.

Miss Arnold's class made paper cones of various sizes, applied the mixture and then poked in sequins, small Christmas balls, wads of tinsel and tiny candles to create their own Christmas trees.

Puppetry. Apples, carrots, green peppers, beets, potatoes, turnips, etc. all make excellent puppet heads. Stick cloves, pins, or thumbtacks, may be used to hold features in place. Colored paper, cloth, feathers, sequins, paint, etc. help make features and trimmings. Finger-sized holes can be bored in the bottom of vegetables or fruit so a finger can be inserted to manipulate the puppet. The insertion of a tongue depressor can serve the same purpose.

Puppetry opens a long avenue of experimentation. Any round or head-shaped object can lend itself to puppetry. Balls (ping-pong or rubber), balloons, wooden knobs, peanuts, paper bags, egg shells, wooden spoons, light bulbs, etc. can become puppet heads, with a little imagination and some scrap materials. Puppets can also be made from paper bags, sticks, papier-mâché or stuffed cloth. Puppetry provides many creative art experiences in the making of the puppets: the stage, the scenery and the costumes.

Peanut shells can be turned into finger puppets. Make caps for each finger from peanut half shells. Draw faces with ink.

Egg Decorations. There are innumerable ways to color Easter eggs. Only a few are listed below:

1. Dipping in dye.
2. Drawing on the egg with colored crayon and then dipping in dye. The dye will not penetrate the crayoned part of the egg.
3. Painting with tempera paint or water color.
4. Placing left-over pieces of crepe paper (or confetti) on a cloth, wrapping the egg in it and dipping it in hot water; the color from the paper dyes the egg.
5. Adding interesting appendages with different kinds of paper, yarn, tin foil, etc.
6. Painting paste designs on the egg and then dipping it in various colored glitter. The glitter sticks to the paste.

Eggs may be blown out by tapping holes in each end with an ice pick and blowing over a bowl. Ribbons may be poked through the eggs and one end can be tied under the egg while the other end of the ribbon can be tied to a branch or to cross sticks, making an egg-mobile.

A branch may be put in a wastebasket of sand and painted so the children can tie on the eggs to make an egg tree.

Hollowed-out eggs may be cut if cuticle scissors are used carefully, thereby making a hole in the egg. The inside of the egg can then be painted and tiny miniature scenes built inside with homemade objects or small miniatures clipped from greeting cards. Rickrack, glitter, sequins and paint can still be used to decorate the outside of the egg.

Papier-mâché eggs may be made by putting strips of paper, dipped in wallpaper paste, over the balloons described on page 82. When the paste is dry the egg can be decorated.

These eggs can also be sliced around the center and opened. Remove the balloon, glue on a strip of cardboard where the egg was cut so it will fit together again. Paint and decorate the inside of the egg and use it as a container for Mother's Easter present which might be some fudge made by the class.

Self Portraits. Encourage each child to do a self portrait using any media. The picture will tell how he sees himself. An interesting variation of this for the primary grades is to have each child lie on a large sheet of wrapping paper on the floor while another child traces his entire outline. Then each child paints in his own features. Miss

Linder used these wrapping-paper figures to fill the seats of the pupils when she had open house for the parents.

Children will also enjoy doing family portraits.

Flannel Board Paintings. Miss Harkness wanted her children to have a group experience in creative composition at Christmas time. She obtained some scrap pieces of red, green and white felt and asked the children to cut out any design that reminded them of the Christmas holiday. They cut stars, trees, ornament shapes, candles, wreaths, Chanukah candles and holly. Miss Harkness then covered a flannel board with white and green flannel. She told the children they were going to paint a flannel picture. She put some Christmas music on the record player and while the music played, each child went to the flannel board and placed his felt pieces in an interesting place. The resulting composition was delightful enough so that the children hung it in the room to enjoy during the Christmas period. The outstanding feature of this project was that the children could change the pieces around or add other pieces to reconstruct the composition. This made a new picture every day.

Egg Carton Art. Papier mâché egg cartons can be cut apart and reassembled into some fascinating forms and shapes. They can be threaded, hung for mobiles, made into package decorations or made into decorations for all occasions. They cut easily, take paint readily and can challenge the children's imagination in putting them to many uses in the classroom.

Melted Crayon Art. The butts of old crayons can be gainfully used in making lovely designs which resemble oil paintings. Put the butts of the same color into the various sections of a cupcake tin and place over a low heat on a hot plate. When the wax is melted, it can be applied as paint to cardboard. The wax cools quickly, giving a thick, glossy finish. It will also adhere to wood and other surfaces. However, caution must be taken to have only a few children sitting around a table working at this at one time for fear of upsetting the warm wax.

Other Ideas

Use materials you collect in the fall to make other ideas or montages.

1. Buy macaroni in as many different shapes as you can find it and see how many things children can do with it.

2. Each day at the front of the class make flower and weed pictures in an old painted frame.

3. Have children use any media they like to make a picture representing *fear, loneliness, pain, anger* or another emotion.

4. Invite someone into the classroom to play a violin or any other musical instrument and ask the children to paint its sound.

5. Present the children with many boxes of drinking straws and common pins. Challenge them to make abstract constructions which will be as tall as possible, which will extend as far as possible from the wall or which will stay suspended in space. This is a challenging problem in construction and gravity.

6. Collect boxes which have unusual textures and surface designs: egg cartons, plastic berry crates or the containers in boxes of chocolates, and see what the children can construct from them. One of the fifth grade boys in Miss Farmer's room made a cluster of beautiful hanging lamps from colored plastic berry boxes.

Summary

Maximum growth in art expression means that the teacher must bring out the child's original ideas and give him the confidence to express them. It means that she must allow art expression to grow out of the child's own experiences so it is vital to him. It means she must understand the level of development of his creative efforts and not pressure him to work beyond his abilities. She must give him a great deal of freedom in making choices and passing judgment and help him to identify and solve problems through the use of art media. Each child should be allowed to find his own way of working, but the teacher can lead him to his potential, and provide him with the skills and knowledge to perfect his work. Art activities should permeate the entire school day and the children must be kept in contact with the beautiful art forms of the world. The work should be evaluated in terms of the children and not in terms of the products they create. The success of a teacher is measured in terms of the creative individuals who leave her class.

TO THE COLLEGE STUDENT

1. You will want to work with art media so you will better understand the creative process in children. Here are some practical situations for you to try your creative abilities.

    a. List all the uses you can think of for a tin can.

    b. Design a file box to hold the materials you are collecting, to be used in your classroom when you do your student teaching. Make it functional but attractive.

    c. Think of all the materials you can which you might use to represent sheep on a mural your students are making.

    d. Buy a cheap straw purse and decorate it. Consider all the possible materials you might use.

    e. Design a card for an ill classmate.

2. Jane Edwards is in the third grade. Every art period Janie sits beside Suzie Kelly and waits to see what Suzie does. Then Janie proceeds to copy it. What is Janie's problem and how would you help her?

3. Look at the environment in which you work daily. What have you done to make it attractive and functional? Do you think environment plays any part in the way people are able to work? Do you think you might be more creative in your college environment if conditions were set daily to help you to create?

4. Discuss this statement in class: It takes more imagination than experience to be able to paint.

5. Laura Zirbes, author of *Spurs to Creative Teaching,* has made some tapes which will stimulate discussion in your class. They may be available in your audio-visual center. The following are suggested for use at this particular time:

No. Z–5   Child Development Through Art Education. 16 min.

No. Z–6   Music and the Creative Urge in Child Development (2 parts), 45 min.

(Source: The Teaching Aids Laboratory, The Ohio State University, Columbus, Ohio).

TO THE CLASSROOM TEACHER

1. Check yourself during a day's time and note how many times you ask your students to follow some pattern—an art pattern, a pattern of thinking or a pattern of doing. Ask yourself how many times this is necessary and how you might better allow the children to

set their minds to work in their own manner. Introduce the children to new ways of thinking and to helping you in new ways of planning.

2. Can your present art program be improved through a realistic team teaching approach? Make a list of all the ways you can work more beneficially with your art teacher.

3. Anna Jones is a kindergarten teacher. During one period she stopped behind Billy Manning's table and held up the crayon drawing on which he was working. "Boys and girls," she said, "I want you all to look at Billy's crayon drawing. Isn't it lovely? See how nicely he has made his flowers. Today he has put petals *and* leaves on his flowers. Last week he didn't have them there. This is so much better, Billy. You are a good boy!"

What is wrong with this situation, considering what you have read in this chapter?

4. Make one creative teaching device to use with your children each day; it need not be elaborate. Try it out and examine your own feelings when you see the children enjoying it. Think of this statement: "To be creative means to care, to care about things and places and human beings. When you care enough about people to do things for them you release creative powers in yourself."

TO THE COLLEGE STUDENT AND THE CLASSROOM TEACHER

1. Examine your own feelings about working in art media. Most adults do not respond positively to situations where they are asked to create with art materials. Why do you think this is so?

2. If each person were really individual, he would dress, talk and be himself. Look at the people around you. Decide which ones are really individuals and which conform to most everything, such as: current hair styles, current clothes styles, accepted behavior in class, use of current slang and speech expressions, status seekers, name droppers, etc. What other factors besides the lack of creative development makes people, especially young adults, become such conformists?

3. What are your reactions to the following situations?

a. Seeing an exhibit of children's paintings defaced by the scribblings of a college student.

b. Having tawdry posters nailed on trees all over the college campus.

c. Seeing a man wearing tan slacks, a brown coat and a dark blue tie.

d. Seeing someone throw a pocketbook in front of a lovely flower arrangement.

e. Seeing circus posters pasted over the glass of a beautiful building.

f. Looking at the window of the average five and ten cent store.

g. Seeing a heavy girl in tight slacks.

Discuss these feelings. Do you think the answers to these questions might help you analyze your own aesthetic sensitivities?

SELECTED BIBLIOGRAPHY

BARKAN, MANUEL. *A Foundation for Art Education.* New York: Ronald Press Co., 1955.

BARKAN, MANUEL. *Through Art to Creativity.* Boston: Allyn and Bacon, Inc., 1960.

COLE, NATALIE. *The Arts in the Classroom.* New York: John Day, 1940.

D'AMICO, VICTOR. *Creative Teaching in Art.* Scranton, Pennsylvania: International Text Book Company, 1953.

DEWEY, JOHN. *Art as Experience.* New York: G. P. Putnam's Sons, 1934.

ERDT, MARGARET H. *Teaching Art in the Elementary School.* New York: Holt, Rinehart and Winston, Inc., 1954.

GAITSKELL, CHARLES D. *Children and Their Art: Methods for the Elementary School.* New York: Harcourt, Brace and World, Inc., 1958.

JEFFERSON, BLANCHE. *Teaching Art to Children.* Boston: Allyn and Bacon, Inc., 1959.

LANDIS, M. *Meaningful Art Education.* Peoria, Illinois: Chas. A. Bennet Co., Inc., 1951.

LOWENFELD, VIKTOR. *Your Child and His Art.* New York: Macmillan Co., 1957.

MANLEY, SEON. *Adventures in Making: The Romance of Crafts Around the World.* New York: The Vanguard Press, 1959.

MATTIL, EDWARD L. *Meaning in Crafts.* Englewood Cliffs, New Jersey: Prentice-Hall, Inc., 1959.

PERRINE, V. D. *Let the Child Draw.* New York: Frederick A. Stokes, 1936.

Creative Teaching Through Music

I shall use the term creativity as a statement of process in the individual: to the extent that a person makes, invents, thinks of something that is new to him; he may be said to have performed a creative act.[1]

MARGARET MEAD

TO THE READER

Do you play the piano? Did you ever take lessons? If so, how well do you play? Many people who took piano when they were young (and some for many years) still cannot play. Why is this so? Discuss this in class or with your colleagues. How did the method by which it was taught influence your ability? From the basic principles of creativity you have already read about, describe how you might teach piano creatively. Then read this chapter. When you have finished, reconsider your own plan. Did you get any ideas you could adapt to your plan?

Introduction

A common objective for teaching music in the elementary school is to develop a love and appreciation of music. Another is to develop skill and mastery of some instrument or some phase of musical accomplishment. While these are important they are not enough. One of the main purposes for including music in the elementary school curriculum is to provide *all* children with a creative means of communication and an outlet for their creative drives. The fulfillment of this objective may well be the best way to accomplish the others.

The music program in the elementary school is designed for *all* children and not solely for those who already appear to have musical ability or a wide background of experiences in music. While individual differences in ability must be met and individual skills developed, conditions in the classroom must be such that all children

[1] Margaret Mead, "Creativity in Cross-Cultural Perspective," in *Creativity and Its Cultivation,* ed. Harold H. Anderson (New York: Harper & Row, Publishers, Inc., 1959), pp. 222–23.

FIGURE 5–1. *A good music center stimulates five-year-olds to experiment and explore sound, and to create their own melodies.*

are provided with equal opportunity for creative development through musical expression. Setting conditions for developing creativity through music will include the following considerations.

There will be many musical materials available in the classroom

If children are to explore and develop musical techniques, a classroom environment must be established which will provide an opportunity for this through the ample use of materials and a well-planned classroom program which provides a wealth of musical experiences for them.

A music center in a classroom should contain materials which challenge children to explore on their own. A victrola with a variety of favorite records can be obtained or borrowed; children enjoy sharing their records from home. Simple musical instruments should also be accessible. These can be inexpensive but true to pitch, such as a flutaphone, a simple marimba or a xylophone. Instruments made by the teacher and children should be ready for immediate use. Children can explore musical tones by use of homemade marimbas, pitched glasses of water or pitched flower pots of various sizes. Spikes suspended by strings produce clear bell-like tones when struck by another metal spike. A horseshoe makes a beautiful substitute for a triangle. Castanets can be made with hollow nut shells. Tambourines can be created from the tops of ice cream containers and inexpensive five and ten cent store bells.

A piano should be part of each classroom and some commercial rhythm instruments are also available. There should be a pad of music paper handy in all grades. Many attractive music books should be accessible. Pictures of musical instruments and of musical activities should be on file. If possible, a radio should be added.

Most of these materials need not be expensive. If they are expensive (such as a victrola), the school curriculum may have to be adjusted to meet the needs of several groups. A victrola or piano may have to be placed on rollers so that it can be easily shared with other groups, but this need be little detriment to the music program if the teacher utilizes the materials at hand to their best advantage. Children should be given a great deal of opportunity to explore the instruments by themselves, and to find out the many sounds and combinations of sounds they can make with them. This does not mean each classroom must be in a constant state of noisy confusion, but that some time should be set aside or some organization planned whereby all children can use music materials without infringing on the rights of privacy of others.

There Must Be a Continual Program of Experiences Which Can Serve as Stimuli for Musical Interpretation

The child's musical experience is based on his own development, his particular needs and interests or his particular feelings. As in art, the subject matter is constantly changing and differs at various age levels, as well as from generation to generation. The child entering kindergarten today has, as a whole, much more contact with music through television, radio, phonograph and the moving picture than the child of a generation ago. He has probably seen more band concerts, attended more musical festivals and seen and heard music used in more ways than children of previous generations. The school curriculum must, therefore, be constantly changing. We teach nursery rhymes and jingles to many children in the kindergarten today at the expense of boring those who, having already learned them at home or in nursery school, are ready for more enriching experiences. One purpose of school is to economically transmit culture, and not to hold children back from learning in any area. Each teacher should know each child's home and background experiences so that he does not run the risk of overemphasizing areas the child already knows and thwarting his drive to move forward.

A three-year-old sat watching a rendition of scenes from *Carmen* before a television set. A famous opera star was singing the arias and dancing the choreography. For one whole hour the three-year-old sat spellbound watching the performance and then said, "That was a good play. Pretty music, too."

Two-year-old children who have had access to many books and whose parents often read and sing to them, quickly recognize words as symbols and will begin to hum when they see a staff with notes on it. At this very early age, the child already has the concept of recorded music and music symbolism.

The subject matter utilized in the music for the young child is a representation of the world around him. Children like to sing about everything they see and hear. They are very responsive to noises and will practice making noises in certain rhythmical patterns in all sorts of ways if given the opportunity. A little girl walks up and down the pavement, up and down the floor, up and down the stairs, up and down, up and down and she says, "Hear the pretty noise my shoes make, Mummy." Children sing sentences to tunes, and hum tunes as they work or play. These are our cues for determining the music curricula.

In art expression, children paint their world and in music they sing about it. As the boundaries of this world expand, so do their interests. Thus the subject matter for the music program is always expanding. As interests and ideas develop, the techniques for teaching music expand also and more and more children learn to use the tools of music. Music experiences in the classroom should be planned so the psychological and physiological needs of children are developed. A third grade class may be very interested in folk music, and a fifth grade class may be interested in Indian music, but the eighth grade or high school boy is apt to be more interested in rock and roll. By experiencing all sorts of music at the time when the child is most receptive, he learns to evaluate and to understand it.

Just as a good art program grows from the experiences of children from day to day and is correlated with their studies and life outside of school, so does a good music program relate to all areas of the curriculum and all facets of life.

For instance, the group of children who studied Mexico (see Chapter II), also experienced a great many interesting musical activities as a result of their interest in Mexico. Some are listed here to show how the immediate interests of the children can provide rich subject matter for musical experiences if the teacher capitalizes on them.

Some Experiences Arising From a Unit

1. The class learned to sing some Mexican songs (some in parts).
   a. They made up and learned some Mexican dances to go with the songs. (Example: "The Hat Dance")

   (1.) "Buy My Tortillas"
   (2.) "Celito Lindo"
   (3.) "The Pearl"
   (4.) "The Samba"
   (5.) "The Dove"

2. The class learned to sing some songs in Spanish:

   (1.) "Palapala"
   (2.) "The Samba"

3. The class became interested in the origin and peculiar rhythm of Spanish music. As a result of this they played many Spanish records.

4. The class became interested in the opera *Carmen*. They read the children's version and played the music from *Carmen* on the victrola. They took a trip to see *Carmen* presented by a traveling opera company. They watched Risë Stevens give a performance of *Carmen* over television.

5. They made an exhibit of musical instruments influenced by the Spanish, for example:

   castanets (made from nut shells) and
   tambourines (made from bells and ice cream keg tops).

6. They learned some ancient Aztec songs and created an Aztec dance in costume.

7. They learned to conga and samba to the music of Xavier Cugat.

8. They learned to play Mexican songs on flutaphones.

9. The class wrote songs on Mexico.

10. They used their Mexican music and dances in a program which they presented, at their fiesta, to the rest of the school.

As in the art experiences resulting from this unit, these rich musical experiences were possible only because the children had been skillfully introduced and guided into a whole new world of unknown experiences. No predetermined course of study could have produced experiences with such meaning. They greatly enriched the life of each child and the techniques used in developing them built good attitudes toward music.

Music often presents placement problems such as where to teach music symbols formally, where to teach the reading of music and where to do part singing. These problems have sometimes been answered by setting lessons at a certain grade level and teaching them religiously *regardless of the readiness, interests or abilities of the children concerned.*

The value of teaching sight reading to children has been often debated. To deprive children of any experience that promotes their growth or understanding of their culture is questionable. Obviously these skills should be taught, but to teach them in a fixed pattern at a fixed time is certainly not the way to help each child grow to maturity, neither in musical abilities nor in creative development. A better plan is to set conditions in the classroom so that learning follows naturally.

There are many instances in a child's life when he should sing for the sheer joy of singing. Music for music's sake is always the desirable outcome of any music program. Each teacher should develop a reservoir of songs children love to sing and use them as much as possible—just for the fun of singing together. She should also know of many recordings children hear, simply because they are delightful. Musical experiences just for enjoyment and satisfaction should be a part of the subject matter of any school's program.

*The Emotional Tone of the Classroom Must
Encourage Musical Experimentation*

A kindergarten teacher had a little boy who brought a beautiful colored leaf to school one autumn day. He showed his leaf to the rest of the group and the class discussed it. They noted and identified its color and its shape and talked about the reasons for its change in color at the change of seasons. The teacher guided the discussion into the life story of the leaves—how the warm sun and soft rain helped them to grow from spring buds and burst through their shells. They talked of how they unfolded and spread out to the warm sunlight, and how they hung trembling from the branches. They talked of how the storms of summer tossed the leaves about and the heat made them limp, and how when the fall came the leaves changed in color and finally came fluttering to the ground where they lay covered by the winter's soft snow. Then they were either raked up and burned or brought to school by some little boy.

As the discussion progressed, the teacher suggested that they play out the story. Various children pretended they were leaves. One little boy curled up on the floor, then began to uncurl and then stretched; he was the bud opening in the warm sun. Both teacher and children admired this interpretation and then asked that he do it again. This time teacher turned to the piano and accompanied his movements with piano rhythms. The children all clapped as his actions were put to music. Teacher asked if someone else would like to play something about a leaf. A little girl stood up and, holding her hands above her head, she pitched and tossed her body about. She was the leaf in the summer storm. Teacher played some storm music to go with her actions. Other children played that they were rain falling on the leaves; some were the leaves falling to the ground; others curled up like leaves under the snow. One creative idea lead to another and the teacher accompanied the children's rhythms with appropriate music.

Finally she taught the children a song about leaves. While they were still expressing enjoyment over the song, five-year-old William said, "I have a song about a leaf." Teacher asked him to tell the group, so he sang Musical Example 1.

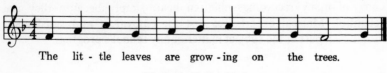

The lit - tle leaves are grow - ing on   the trees.

Musical Example 1

"Isn't that lovely!" said teacher. "Let's all sing Bill's song." So she picked out the tune on the piano and they all sang it. Karen said, "I could sing a song, too."

"Good," said the teacher, "that goes right along with Bill's song—let's sing them both together," so they sang both lines of the song (Musical Example 2).

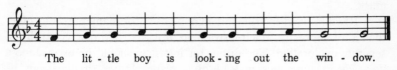

The lit - tle boy is look - ing out the win - dow.

Musical Example 2

Other lines were added until the song was complete.

Teacher then picked out the song on the piano. "I guess I'd better write down our song," she said, "so I can play it again and again and not forget it." She took some lined paper from the piano and made the notes on the staff. "This is the way you write music," she said.

Other experiences of this nature produced similar songs until a book appropriately titled *Our Songs* sat on the piano with a gay cover painted by a child. The book was used daily when the class sang its favorite songs.

These children were living creative experiences in a relaxed, creative environment. The rhythms were created first; the music served to show how feeling and action can be interpreted by more than one medium. Creative products resulted from the experience, with the children playing a major role in the creative act. They were not inhibited in their thinking by the demand to fill a set pattern and they had not been forced to be a listening and following audience. Each listened, thought, acted, lead and produced on his own.

Another kindergarten teacher made wise use of the rhythm band. The children listened to a recording of a child's record with a good rhythm. Then rhythm instruments were placed so that the children could choose any one. The teacher played sections of the music and asked individuals in the group to play their instruments to accompany the music. In this way the children produced a variety of rhythms. They learned from each other that there are many ways of interpreting music and using instruments. Some accented each note with bells and tambourines; some kept time with cymbals and triangles; others hit only the after-beat with drums and rhythm sticks. The teacher then suggested that the entire record be played while each child played his instrument. The concert that followed was much more beautiful and creative than the usual accented, to a beat set by the teacher, bang of instruments. A change of instruments promotes further discovery and exploration of new effects. Rhythm bands, used in this manner, encourage the child to interpret and understand music.

Rhythm band instruments may be used for many purposes other than a toy orchestra. Each instrument, if it is a good one, is worthy of separate exploration. The drum, for instance, should be used alone a great deal; sometimes instead of a piano. Drum rhythms can be utilized for certain kinds of rhythm steps which the piano does not inspire. Use of these instruments is not confined to the lower grades. Some third and fourth grade boys created a group of Inca and Aztec dances using their own drum rhythm. This created an unusual effect when danced in costumes and masks. Each rhythm instrument has a unique quality of its own which should lead to an exciting series of experiences.

The creation of music, begun in nursery school and kindergarten, should be continued throughout children's school life. They can soon learn to record their own melodies so others can play them. Using a marimba, xylophone or tuned glasses, children can easily learn to make up tunes and record them with numbers. After each child has had experience with composition of this type, the group may create a song for a school program, and the teacher may utilize this opportunity to teach children how to record music with notes and measures so that anyone can read it, just as she teaches them to write their stories so others may read them. Some first grade teachers have done this simply and with a great deal of success. The time for presenting written music must not depend on a grade level but on the child's having had a wealth of experience in simple composition and recording. If it is taught with meaning, and in the child's own language, it will be understood.

One fifth grade, with a rich musical background, wrote and filmed a motion picture on the history of their community. The class then set out to write a song for the introduction to the film, but became so interested in composing music that they not only wrote songs for the entire film but orchestrations for the songs as well. Members of the class who played musical instruments met with the music teacher and set the score to a musical background.

If young children play simple instruments with success, they desire to continue their exploration. First, rhythm instruments answer the need, then simple instruments such as the flutophone, mouth organ, marimba and ukelele become a challenge which can be met with a great deal of success. In the intermediate grades, more difficult musical instruments claim the attention of the child.

In each step the child should have the opportunity to explore, discover and create with his instrument, for awhile. Then he is ready for help from a teacher who will understand him and lead him into the acquisition of the necessary skills to master the instrument. The teacher helps the child establish a relationship with the instrument—to get the feel of it and find out what he can do with it. He is given simple exercises which assure him of success from the start. Much of the earliest work with instruments should be ear training.

A child need not be bored with monotonous and meaningless drill if each lesson is rich with variety and crowned with a sense of achievement. If a child understands and loves his instrument he will practice, and some of his practice will be with the work he, himself, has written and recorded. The compulsion of the child in the intermediate grades to master skills shows in his desire to play a musical instrument well, and this occurs when he is properly motivated. Success is necessary to continue this motivation; too many unresolved failures may cause a child to abandon his instrument altogether. Music experiences should always give pleasure and satisfaction to children.

Music Must Be Experienced For Its Aesthetic Values

When the subject matter of music curricula is determined by the interests of the children, they see more meaning in music experiences. Songs, recordings and instruments—are all interesting to children when applied to their natural school life. For this reason, popular music has a definite place in school. With the radio and television so rich with musical programs, children learn to sing many popular songs. Much of popular music is excellent for classroom instruction and children who have had no other musical background can begin here before branching out into other areas of musical exploration. Popular music is something children understand; it is a product of their present culture and can be a springboard to new horizons.

The modern school should attempt to develop the skill of listening (see Book II, *Creative Teaching of the Language Arts in the Elementary School*).[2] Our culture demands more and more that we listen, as well as speak, effectively. Excellent recordings are

[2] James A. Smith, *Creative Teaching of the Language Arts in the Elementary School* (Boston: Allyn and Bacon, Inc., 1967).

available for classroom use; good radio and television programs increase the importance of a good listening audience. Skills for listening to music correspond to the skills for observing art. As a child develops his ability to listen, he develops his responses to sound and a greater appreciation of harmonious composition. He learns not only to hear a beautiful piece of music but to identify the individual instruments which constitute the composition. Through understanding, his appreciation grows. Teachers may guide children in their listening techniques by pointing out details which the children should note. The composition itself must never be destroyed through this technique, however, any more than poetry should be destroyed by picking it to pieces.

As in other good learning situations, the prime factor in developing the concept of music, is experience. The teacher who provides enriching classroom experiences for her children is fairly well-assured of developing creativity and appreciation in them. As a part of the daily program, these situations lead children toward musical maturity. Add to these trips to concerts or good musicals, sharing of fine school assemblies, invitations to people in the community to play for the children, good radio and television programs, and a variety of musical contacts and the music becomes a means of developing creativity in every child.

The Teaching of Music Will Contribute to the Development of the Qualities of Creativity

The teacher will engage children in activities requiring divergent thinking which will result in original products. She will encourage discovery and originality. She will set conditions for teaching music which will bring about a flow of ideas and a joy in playing with and changing these ideas. She will help children redefine and elaborate these ideas. They will identify closely with music as a means of creative expression.

On the following pages, many examples are given to show how various teachers have put these principles into practice, and used convergent thinking to create new products. Some examples show how teachers developed creative responses in children by giving them basic principles with which to operate. All of the examples show the importance of the manipulation of materials, tools, words and ideas in arriving at the creative product. Some simply show how teachers have built a sensitivity to music as a creative communicative media.

Suggestions for Setting Conditions for Primary Music Activities

The child beginning school is concerned with himself and his immediate world. Kindergarten is his second home, the kindergarten teacher is his second mother. He is active and his attention span is short. He is interested more in *doing* than in the *result* of his doing. Music is natural to him and manifests itself in the rhythm of all he does. He likes to experiment with sound and with his body, and to repeat things he has learned. Music should be present from time to time throughout his day.

Many of the activities suggested on the following pages contribute to other aspects of the curriculum besides music. Concepts of high and low, tall and short and heavy and light are a necessary concept for reading readiness and may be developed creatively through the music program. Following is how one first grade teacher developed the concepts of high and low, heavy and light, big and small, happy and sad and at the same time developed the children's creative abilities.

Miss Parker took her first grade to the zoo. After the children returned to the classroom, they discussed the animals they had seen. Pictures of the animals were mounted and labeled, and the movements of the animals dramatized.

One day, Miss Parker saw an opportunity to develop some abstract concepts in a creative way. She asked the children if they would like to make up an original musical story about an animal who went to the zoo. She structured the story in that she suggested that the animal be a rabbit, since it is the only animal who does not make a sound.

Janet suggested that the rabbit might go to the zoo in search of a sound he could make. Everyone liked Janet's idea so Miss Parker developed the story from this point on.

The elephant was the first animal that Mr. Rabbit met.

"We have used the piano a great deal for singing and dancing," said Miss Parker, "now listen carefully while I play each key. You tell me then which keys make the high sounds and which keys make the low sounds."

The children identified the high keys and the low keys and then Miss Parker asked, "Now tell me, what do you remember about the elephant? Was he big or little? Light or heavy?"

Of course, the children responded in a chorus, "Big! Heavy!"

"Johnny, you show me with your hands how the elephant walks."

Johnny put the heel of his hand on the floor and heavily pressed on it until the fingers also touched the floor, then he proceeded to walk his hands along the floor.

"Good," encouraged Miss Parker. "Now children, where would Johnny put his hands on the keys to show that the elephant walks slow and heavy?"

The children pointed to the proper end of the keyboard. "Heavy sounds can be made with the low notes then, can't they?" said Miss Parker. "Johnny, come to the piano and walk your hands on the low notes just as you did on the floor and we will see if it sounds like an elephant."

The children were delighted at the result. "Well, what animal will Mr. Rabbit meet next? Can you think of one where we might use the high notes?"

The deer was suggested. Paula made her fingers play over the high keys in a dainty, dignified manner. The children added the kangaroo next who bounced over the heavy keys to the medium range and back again. Soon many animals were represented by music. The children suggested the rabbit should have a musical theme too. Mary made her fingers hop the whole length of the keyboard and back again.

The story was ready to put together. One child told how Mr. Rabbit set out on a trip to the zoo to find a sound he could make. First he came to Mr. Elephant (at this point, Johnny played the elephant music) but he decided he didn't like the elephant's sound so he went on until he met Miss Deer (Paula then played deer music), and the story continued.

An amusing twist came in the story when Jimmy suggested the ending. Jimmy said, "The zoo is so noisy, let's have all the animals make their noises at the same time, then Mr. Rabbit will go home 'cause he's glad it's so quiet at home."

No sooner was this said than the creative musical story was complete. Concepts were taught meaningfully and the divergent powers of the children were teased.

Primary children enjoy the following activities which lay a foundation for forms of creative expression:

Learn, by Rote to Sing

1. Songs about home, school, neighborhood.
2. Songs with special phrases to help child find his singing voice.
3. Excerpts from songs that older children sing.
4. Nonsense or fun songs.
5. Songs with actions.
6. Songs that suggest movement and dramatization.
7. Songs that children make up about everyday experiences.
8. Songs of the seasons and special days.

Move to Music

1. That suggests walking, running, skipping, galloping.
2. That suggests dramatizations in singing games.
3. For free and individual interpretive response.
4. For clapping.
5. That allows child to respond at his own tempo.
6. That suggests animal movements: the lumbering of an elephant, the waddle of the duck.
7. That suggests mood: show happiness, show loneliness, etc.
8. That suggests abstractions: show water, be a wheel, etc.
9. That encourages original dance patterns.

Play

1. Simple instruments to accompany songs.
2. Sand blocks for train songs.
3. Rhythm sticks for clock songs.
4. Rhythm band instruments.
5. Bells.
6. Mouth organs.
7. Drums to accompany creative dances.
8. Musical games.

Listen

1. To teacher or a visitor play the piano, violin or other instrument.
2. To others sing a beautiful song.
3. To learn a new song.
4. To dramatize a story to music.
5. To begin to establish good listening habits.
6. To children's records.
7. To radio programs.
8. To musical television programs.

Develop

1. An awareness of up and down in music.
2. An awareness of high and low.
3. An awareness of loud and soft.
4. A feeling for steady rhythm. (These contribute to music reading readiness)
5. A love for music.
6. A knowledge of instruments.
7. Creative songs and dances.

Explore and Discover

1. Different-sized bells for different tones.
2. The piano and its possibilities.
3. The possibility of making different sounds on a drum (big and small drums; sides, rims, as well as heads to play on).
4. The possibility of melody instruments for creating, as well as accompanying, songs (tone blocks, melody bells).
5. Through actual contact, things of interest about instruments brought in by teacher or visitors.
6. The possibility of scarves or light material to represent creative rhythms. (Bells sewn on elastics worn on ankles to symbolize trotting ponies, for example).

Use the Body with Music

1. Dance with scarves, capes, ribbons, ropes, bells and similar materials, to creative rhythms and dramatizations.

Play Simple Instruments

1. Autoharp
2. Harmolin
3. Rhythm instruments—sticks, sand blocks, drums, etc.
4. Simple melody instruments—"tone blocks," etc.
5. Piano and a good phonograph
6. Flutophone
7. Marimba
8. Mouth organ

Making musical instruments at all grade levels can develop children's observation and listening powers. Both of these skills are a basis for artistic expression. Such an activity can grow out of a unit on "sound" in the intermediate grades where children listen to all kinds of combinations of materials to produce new sounds and to discover which materials carry sound and which do not. All kinds of small objects (thumb tacks, paper clips, pebbles, macaroni, rice, sand and glass) can be enclosed in hollow containers (boxes, gourds, tin pie plates, paper plates and old balls) to test for new sounds. Sound stories and musical compositions may be invented from the products of such experimentation. In activities such as these, children learn through discovery and create with what they discover.

Among the basic principles of creative teaching is that creative teaching initiates self-learning, stresses convergent thinking *and* divergent thinking, allows children to manipulate and explore materials and develops uniqueness and individuality.

All of these principles can be employed when children create their own instruments. The following list is only a springboard to the many ideas children will have once they begin to invent with sounds.

CLICKING INSTRUMENTS

Rhythm sticks	doweling of small diameter cut in 12-inch lengths (hard wood is best)
Wood blocks	sections of an old baseball bat
Temple blocks	sections of an old bowling pin
Claves	paired resonant sticks; six-inch sections of an old broomstick
Coconut shells	split coconut shells; two paper cups struck together produce a softer sound

RINGING INSTRUMENTS

Triangles	horse shoes or suspended large nails
Chimes	suspended silver spoons of different sizes; resonant curtain rods
Gong	length of iron pipe; old brake drums; one cymbal
Cymbals	resonant metal covers; brass trays
Tambourines	heavy cardboard pie plates with bottle caps, roofing disks, or sea shells attached near the rim; embroidery hoops
Jingle sticks	jingling metal disks (disks used in roofing or bottle caps) fastened loosely on a stick

SWISHING INSTRUMENTS

Maracas (shakers or rattles)	gourds with seeds or pebbles inside; various containers with chalk, gravel or peas inside (mounted on handles if desired); medicine bottles with rice; clam shells with shot; old light bulbs covered with papier-mâché (when dry, break glass by rapping sharply on table)

Drums

chopping bowls, wooden kegs, lard cans, and waste baskets with calfskin or heavy rubber thumbtacked, nailed, or laced on. Smaller ones may be made from oatmeal boxes or other cardboard containers used as they are or with ends covered with a rubber sheet.

Things to do with rhythm instruments:

1. Make up a story and use percussion instruments for sound effects. Example: The alarm clock (triangle) awakes us in the morning. The clock (gong) strikes eight. Mother calls, "Are you sleeping?" (Sing the song to the accompaniment of the clock ticking-woodblocks, rhythm sticks). On the way to school we hear a train (sandblocks) and horses (coconut shells). Such a story is another way to teach the appropriateness of individual percussion instruments.

2. Practice some "drum talk." During this activity, the drum plays the rhythm of words or names. One variant of this consists of the teacher beating the rhythm of words or parts of a familiar song on a drum, and the children answering by playing instruments or clapping the rhythm of answering words. Example for primary grades:

Teacher drums:	"Mary had a little lamb."
Children:	"Little lamb, little lamb."
Teacher:	"Mary had a little lamb."
Children:	"Its fleece was white as snow."

3. Make up a story around one instrument (the drum is especially good for this). Then play records of stories which use one instrument. (Example: "Little Indian Drum," Young Peoples Records)

Other Activities:

1. Children can be stimulated to make up their own songs to accompany simple dramatizations. Musical Example 3 is one teacher's account of how one such song came from a dramatization in Miss Peterson's third grade.

RONALD'S SONG

Musical Example 3

Laurie brought a *Child Life* magazine to school with a pirate play in it and asked if we could "play it." We talked about producing a play. Words like sets, casting, properties and costumes were all discussed. Laurie became the producer and did the casting. Though favoritism played a small part in the casting, we selected voices that the audience would hear easily.

We worked very hard at learning our lines, then decided to tape the play. Teacher prompted the idea of having music. Ronald said he had a song but wouldn't say it out-loud. He whispered it in my ear and the words were set to music to use at the opening of the play. We had a narrator tell the name of the play and list the characters.

Props consisted of two tables pulled together to represent one side of a ship. A plank was propped on two blocks. Billy was in charge of the blocks and the teacher was in charge of getting the tables and plank ready.

Mary decided she didn't want to be a prisoner if she had to walk the plank. We assured her that she wouldn't need to walk the plank because the ship was really run by a pirate who had a big heart.

2. Many children will have older brothers or sisters who can play musical instruments. Invite them to the classroom to perform. Better yet, invite parents who sing or play a musical instrument.

Invite a Boy Scout bugler to play for the children and to tell about his bugle.

3. Singing games are excellent to develop rhythm and to help children feel music; "Mulberry Bush," "Go In and Out the Window," "Looby Lou," "Farmer in the Dell" and many others may be replaced in the intermediate grades by "Brother Come and Dance with Me," "Here I Come, Where From," jump rope songs, folk games and dances.

4. As children walk, skip, jump or march, introduce a rhythmic pattern to show them how their motions would look expressed

musically. For instance, a walk step might look like Musical Example 4.

Musical Example 4

A skipping step might look like Musical Example 5.

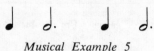

Musical Example 5

These experiences can form a base for reading music later on.

5. Music can aid the child in adjusting to new situations. It can help children to release hostile and negative tensions in positive ways. As a media for promoting good mental health it belongs in the category of the socio-drama and other socio-dynamic devices explored in Book IV, chapt. XII.[3] A book by Lydia Fern Tallmadge, William H. Tallmadge and Francis M. Wilson called, "Sing Trouble Away" (New York Teachers Library, 1790 Broadway, New York 19, N.Y., 1957) contains songs and accompanying suggestions for helping children release tensions through music.

6. Sing each child's name for roll call and have him respond by repeating the tune or making up one that goes with yours.

7. Children will enjoy listening to special records about single or grouped instruments. Some records of this nature are:

"Tubby the Tuba" (Decca)
"Rusty in Orchestraville" (Capital)
"The Magic Clock" (Young Peoples Records)
"The Wonderful Violin" (Young Peoples Records)
"Said the Piano to the Harpsichord" (Young Peoples Records)
"Licorice Stick" (Young Peoples Records)
"The Little Brass Band" (Young Peoples Records)
"Mr. Grump and Dingle School Band" (Young Peoples Records)
"Strike Up the Band" (Young Peoples Records)
"The King's Trumpet" (Young Peoples Records)
"Big Brass Band and Big Joe the Tuba" (RCA Victor)
"Happy Instruments" (Columbia)
"Official Bugle Calls" (Decca)
"Child's Introduction to the Orchestra" (Golden)
"Lead a Little Orchestra" (Columbia)

[3] ————, *Creative Teaching of the Social Studies in the Elementary School* (Boston: Allyn and Bacon, Inc., 1967).

8. When children create a poem or song and set it to music, and you prepare the final manuscript, use a symbol for the notes which is related to the topic. Example: Musical Example 6.

Musical Example 6

Suggestions for Developing Creativity Through Intermediate Grade Activities

1. As children study various parts of their own country, and other countries, obtain original, authentic songs from each area and sing them. The music will help to develop a "feeling" for a country.

Recordings of folk music from the world over can now be obtained. Some excellent examples are:

"Going West" (Young Peoples Records)
"Chisholm Trail" (Young Peoples Records)
"Christopher Columbus" (Young Peoples Records)
"Yankee Doodle and Other Folk Songs" (Young Peoples Records)
"Maypole Dance" [English Folk Song] (RCA Victor)
"Turn Me; Turn Around Me" [Czech Folk Song] (RCA Victor)
"Wheat" [Czech Folk Song] (RCA Victor)
"Cshebogar" [Hungarian Folk Song] (RCA Victor)
"Tantoli" [Swedish] (RCA Victor)
"Dance of Greeting" [Danish Folk Song] (RCA Victor)
"Ancient and Oriental Music" (RCA Victor)
"Early Medieval Music Up to 1300" (RCA Victor)

2. Collect themes from radio and television programs and trace them back to their origin. Many great pieces of music now provide children with their introduction to TV shows, and are often the first exposure the child has to classical music.

3. Reading music is no problem when children have written their songs in music symbols. The sequence in reading words is: experience, verbal symbol (oral expression), printed symbol (reading), then the writing. In music it is the same. The child experiences, he sings his experience, the teacher prints it with music symbols and he

reads it. Then he is ready to read the music symbols of others. Just as he is given phonic training, so he can become independent in his normal reading activity, he is given help in understanding and using new music symbolism as he encounters it in his reading of music.

4. Part singing may well be preceded by choral speaking where children speak lines of words with sounds to get the feel of putting together different sounds at the same time (see Book II).[4] Soon rounds can be introduced. Children can experience part-singing first by using their own songs or poems and chanting different tunes at the same time in their dramatizations or by using sound stories.

5. Children in the intermediate grades enjoy experimenting with making musical instruments. They can go beyond the realm of tuned glasses and flower pots and make stringed instruments by stretching rubber bands of varied thickness and tension over the open ends of cigar boxes, or stringing wires or cat gut over frames. Children in these grades can make respectable wooden marimbas, glass or metal xylophones and various kinds of drums. Often these instruments can be made in association with a science unit on the topic of sound.

6. One of the most creative approaches to music is the method developed by Carl Orff and his assistant Gunild Keltman. In Mr. Orff's approach, no highly developed instruments are used and children are free to express themselves fully. The purpose of the method is to develop in children a sense of rhythm, form, melody, beauty of sound, the spoken word and humor. Mr. Orff's work with children has been put on recordings and may be purchased through Angel Records, New York City. [Carl Orff and Gunild Keltman, *Music for Children,* Album 3582-B (35650–651)]. Mr. Orff's work is inspiringly creative.

7. Children in the intermediate grades enjoy making up songs to accompany cheers for their favorite basketball or football teams.

Mrs. Pomeroy, a music consultant,[5] used as many opportunities as possible to help children in her classes understand that life around them could be translated into musical expression. The children at each grade level used appropriate experiences to create music. They wrote songs about everything constantly, both through group experiences and individually. Some of the topics Mrs. Pomeroy used were:

[4] ———, *Setting Conditions for the Creative Teaching of the Language Arts in the Elementary School* (Boston: Allyn and Bacon, 1967).

[5] Special acknowledgement for these materials must be made to Mrs. Sally Algiers Pomeroy, music teacher of the Lafayette Central School and Liverpool Central Schools, New York 1955–1958.

"A Spooky Night"
"Thanksgiving Is Coming"
"Thanksgiving Is a Thankful Day"
"Gobbley, Gobbley"
"Fall"
"Spring"
"Winter Song"
"Snowflakes"
"The Wind"
"The Hoptoad"
"Be My Valentine"
"The Fisherman Song"
"We'll Sail for a Whale"
"Dolly's Sandman"
"Ann's Trip"
"A Ride on a Horse"
"Baseball and Me"
"Two Cents to Spend"

"The Harvest Song"
"Fun in Winter"
"It's Fun to Go Sliding"
"A Summer Surprise"
"I Make a Snowman"
"I Like Winter"
"Robin Redbreast"
"Beautiful Rainbow"
"When Santa Comes"
"A New Pet"
"We Make Valentines"
"Policeman Bill"
"The Five Little Fish"
"The Aeroplane"
"Happy Boys and Girls"
"The Football Game"
"Oil on Puddles"
"The Sky at Night"

Musical Examples 7, 8 and 9 are some sample songs written by her classes, and by her individual students.

THE FALL SONG

by Mrs. Abbey's Second Grade

The leaves are dif-ferent col-ors, The leaves are fal-ling down,

When-e-ver I go out The leaves are on the ground!

Musical Example 7

AUTUMN WEATHER

by Patricia Suters, Grade 2

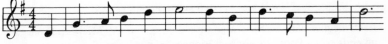

I like the au-tumn wea-ther, the days are crisp and cold.

I have to wear a swea-ter, the leaves are red and gold.

Musical Example 8

WE MAKE VALENTINES
by Mrs. Knock's Second Grade

We make val - en - tines and give them a - way.

Let's make some val - en - tines to - day.

We make val - en - tines, red and white.

They are bright and a won - der - ful sight!

Musical Example 9

Mrs. Pomeroy's fourth grade children wrote some songs about their local heroes. Here is one (Musical Example 10).

The children enjoyed writing fun songs, also, as Musical Example 11 shows.

Often the children in Mrs. Pomeroy's classes loved tunes (especially folk tunes) so much that they hummed them much of the time. Mrs. Pomeroy heard them making up new words to go with these old tunes, so she encouraged the children to develop this idea. Here are some samples of the work she received from the children:

New verses to "OLD MICHAEL FINNEGAN"

(Each begins with "There was an old man named Michael Finnegan" and ends with "Poor old Michael Finnegan!")

He played tennis with his chinnegan
He knocked the ball from here to Minnegan. (Third Grade)

He grew up to be a man again
He grew down to a little boy again.   (Fourth Grade)

THE FOURTH GRADE HERO

by Mrs. Stneb's Fourth Grade

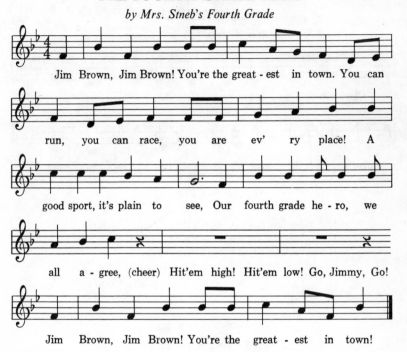

Jim Brown, Jim Brown! You're the great - est in town. You can run, you can race, you are ev' ry place! A good sport, it's plain to see, Our fourth grade he - ro, we all a - gree, (cheer) Hit'em high! Hit'em low! Go, Jimmy, Go! Jim Brown, Jim Brown! You're the great - est in town!

Musical Example 10

He had a car and smashed it in again
He bought a new one and turned it in again. (Third Grade)

He ate an apple with a spoonegan
Then he grew apples out of his earsegan!   (Third Grade)

GOLDEN GOLD

Tune: Sweet Betsey from Pike

O California here I come
With a washbowl on my thumb,
We crossed the plains, the mountains and hills
And all we ate was vitamin pills!

O I came in search of golden gold
All my pockets would ever hold,
All we did was wash rocks and soil,
O why do we have to do all this toil.

CLARABELLE

by Mrs. Lardeo's Second Grade

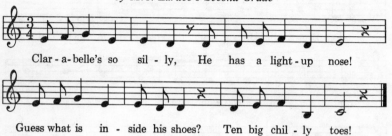

Clar - a- belle's so   sil - ly,   He   has   a   light - up   nose!

Guess what is   in - side his shoes?   Ten big chil - ly   toes!

Musical Example 11

I found a few nuggets worth thousands of dollars
We got all that money in just a few hours,
It was lucky we had those vitamin pills
Or the Indians would have put us in kilns!

by Mrs. Coon's
Fifth Grade

PANNING FOR GOLD

Tune: Working on the Railroad

I've been panning for gold
All the live-long day,
I've been panning for gold
And washing the dirt away,
Today I found a golden nugget
Yesterday I found four,
And when I go tomorrow
I'll find a whole lot more.

Been panning for gold
Been panning for gold,
Been panning for gold all day.
(Repeat)

Someone up-stream with my partner
Someone up-stream I know,
Someone up-stream with my partner
Trying to buy some gold
And singing
I've come west to get gold
In the cold mountain stream,

I've come west to get gold
But I'll never get rich it seems.

by The Trio, Mrs. Wayand's
Fifth Grade

THE BIG BASS FIDDLE
by Mrs. Smith's Third Grade

Musical Example 12

THE RETREATING FLUTOPHONE
by Robert Woodruff, Grade 4

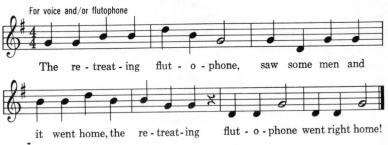

Musical Example 13

Mrs. Pomeroy's pupils explored each musical instrument carefully once they reached the fourth grade. They learned to identify the
instruments and their sounds. The unique sounds of each instrument
led the children to write songs about them. Musical Examples 12, 13
and 14 are some written by groups and individuals.

When a special event came around, Mrs. Pomeroy tried to catch
the flavor of the children's interest by finding songs which went well

MY PIANO

by Kathleen Reilly, Grade 5

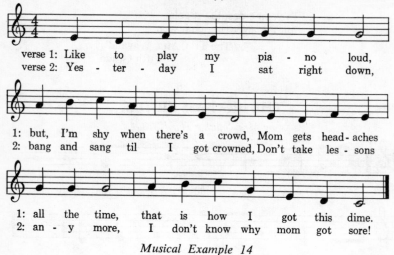

verse 1: Like to play my pia - no loud,
verse 2: Yes - ter - day I sat right down,

1: but, I'm shy when there's a crowd, Mom gets head-aches
2: bang and sang til I got crowned, Don't take les - sons

1: all the time, that is how I got this dime.
2: an - y more, I don't know why mom got sore!

Musical Example 14

with the particular occasion. After singing "Take Me Out to the Ball Game," the children in the sixth grade wanted to write their own World Series song. They decided they would use the tune of "Take Me Out to the Ball Game" because they were so fond of it. They called their creation "The Series Song," with half the class rooting for one team and half rooting for the other.

THE SERIES SONG

Tune: Take Me Out To The Ball Game

The Yankees are a good ball team
But the Dodgers are sure to win
Our pitchers are better than Yankee ones
Campy and Snider are hitting home runs
And it's root, root, root for the Dodgers
If they don't win it's a shame
So it's one, two, three more home runs
And the ball game is won!

Take me out to the Yanks
For they're the highest in ranks
Buy me some peanuts and red hot franks
We'll watch the series, the Dodgers and Yanks
Root, root, root for the Yankees
For they're the very best team
So it's six, seven, eight, nine, ten
And the Yanks are winning again!

by Mrs. Sloper's
Sixth Grade

Mrs. Pomeroy also had a knack for turning catastrophe into fun. During the rage for calypso music, the teacher faced a problem in showing a film. She used the occasion to develop a calypso song with the children.

WHAT HAPPENED TO THE MOVIE?

Verse: One day we had a movie
The film was put in wrong.
When she started the projector
We laughed loud and long.

Chorus: The funny movie!
The funny movie!
What happened to it?
What happened to it?

by Miss Mann's
Fifth Grade

Mrs. Pomeroy often encouraged the children to write about music. She often took a musical instrument to class for the children to observe and try. After the experience, many children wrote creative stories and poems around the classes. Some of the topics suggested were:

The Story of a Tuba
The Sound of a Tuba Reminds Me of: . . .
The Tuba and the Piccolo
Fatty the Flute
The Sound of Music

The following stories show some of the children's responses to this sort of stimuli:

ALFRED THE TUBA

Once upon a time, there was this Tuba who was very lonely. He wanted to play in a band. His friends all teased him.

One day this band came to town and Alfred said this may be my chance, so he went over and they said they would try him out. They tried and tried and tried. But no noise would come out. The manager said he would have to be cleaned out.

So Alfred went to the Annette Music School. They tried to clean him out but they just couldn't. Alfred was so sad that he began to cry. He cried and cried and cried and he cleaned himself out. The first thing he did was go to the band and the manager said, "You are in!" From that day on Alfred was never lonely again.

by Diane, Grade 3

FINICKY THE FLUTE

I am a flute. My name is Finicky, the Flute. I am here to tell you what happens to me when Carol plays me.

First of all, I must tell you that I belong to the woodwind family. My nice sweet tone is produced by a current of air blown into my mouthpiece. My greatgrandmother was once played by blowing into the top of a mouthpiece like a clarinet. The Greeks and Hebrews played this way. I now am a long tube. I have a little hole into which you blow. I have many keys which you push down to make different sounds. My brother is a piccolo. He is much shorter than I am because he didn't eat his Wheaties. He also has a higher sound than I do. We are both in the orchestra and band.

by Linda, Grade 5

POLLY, THE PIANO

Polly was a piano. She was a very unhappy piano. When you touched her key it would hit the string and go "bong." She was out of tune and no one could fix her. The reason she was out of tune was because she was unhappy, but no one knew that.

One day a little girl and her mother came into the warehouse where Polly was. It was a warehouse for pianos. They said to the manager, "We would like to see a pretty piano." They looked at many pianos, but they couldn't find a pretty piano like they were looking for.

Then, all at once, the little girl named Ruth said, "Mommy, look! Here is a very cute piano."

The manager said, "Yes, she is very cute, but some of her piano keys aren't in tune—"

"Oh, we can get someone to fix her," said Ruth. "Please can we get her?"

Finally her mother said it would be all right. So they bought Polly. Now Polly was happy and they found out that she could play well, but they never found out why she wouldn't play in tune in the warehouse.

by Lois, Grade 5

Mrs. Pomeroy helped her children learn about composers of beautiful music. They read stories about them and gave reports or dramatizations of their lives. Many children went to see moving pictures about the lives of these composers and later made reports about them to the class. The children became so interested in the composers that they drew pictures and wrote poems about them.

Poems About FRANZ JOSEPH HAYDEN

Franz J. Haydn
Had something inside him,
Most men did not have in mind

To birds he must have been kind.
In a cathedral he did play,
Making a living day by day
On a violin he did plink, plink, plink,
But making symphonies he did think, think, think.

*   *   *

Papa Haydn
When a boy
Used to have a little toy
He called it a violin.
It went everywhere with him.
A very busy man was he
Didn't even stop to have his tea.
He wrote music oh so grand,
Even when he was an old man.

*   *   *

Franz J. Haydn was so very good,
He wrote music as no one could.
He loved to sing and dance so well,
He went away to play a spell.
He loved to play his violin,
Singing and dancing went well with him.
He finally went to play in a symphony,
And this is what made him really happy.

Mrs. Pomeroy encouraged her children to write limericks inspired by musical sounds and musical instruments.

LIMERICKS

There was a monkey who was a pet,
He was very good on the clarinet,
He played for his master,
Until a disaster,
Ruined his lovely clarinet!

*   *   *

There was a fish called a carp,
Who was exceedingly good on a harp,
He played for his brother,
And also for his mother,
And all of them liked his harp.

by Patty, Grade 5

*   *   *

There once was a lady from Malone,
Who played on a big saxaphone,

She blew up like a balloon,
And out came a sweet tune,
Now she plays in the concerts back home.

by Peggy, Grade 5

Often, Mrs. Pomeroy would use recordings to help develop musical appreciation or musical interpretation. One of her favorite devices was to play a record and give these simple instructions: "Write whatever the music makes you think of." Here are some of the results:

from YOUNG PERSON'S GUIDE TO THE ORCHESTRA
(*Second Grade Impressions*)

"Makes me sleepy. A happy day. Sad. Someone died. Makes me dance. Someone in love. A Birthday. Makes me fly in the air. Makes me float. Run to the store. Very happy. The bride."

*   *   *

I love music. It is loud and soft. It has drums and instruments. It can be real soft and sometimes makes you sleepy. It will remind you of many things. It will make you think you're beautiful. It will go slow and then scare you by going fast all of a sudden, and it will play real loud and then sound like it stopped, but it just gets real soft. It will make you sleep forever like I was doing tonight. Now while the harp is playing with that lovable piano, the band will play so soft you'll cry when you sleep.

THE LITTLE RAINDROP

Once upon a time there was a little raindrop. Her name was Nan. She lived up in the heavens. Every time God made it rain Nan always ran to the open part of the clouds. But every time she got there the rain was over. The whole world was dry as could be. Now one day, as Nan was running to the open part of the clouds, suddenly she fell down, down, down, right to the ground. The other raindrops cheered and cheered. Because Nan fell to the ground all at once. They were so happy that they crowned Nan and made her princess of raindrops. She married George raindrop. So they were prince and princess. Now they are all very happy together. Nan had some children. A little boy and girl, Tom and Carol. And they are all happy. Tom and Carol play all the time. And they lived happily ever after.

by Linda

Mrs. Pomeroy introduced rhythm instruments to her first grade, one pupil at a time. She first used one of the most interesting instruments, the triangle. Most of the children had played the triangle

in kindergarten, but by only one method. Her experiments to
many ways she could hold and use the triangle provided a repertoire
of sound effects and ideas. Experiments in the upper grades sometimes started with sounds and then fitted appropriate instruments to
them, as in the sounds of Halloween.

THE WONDERFUL TRIANGLE

The first graders experimented with the triangle. They discovered
that it can make many different sounds if it is held in various ways. Here
are some of the things the triangle reminded them of.

Soft Sounds

little baby's feet	Tinker Bell
prayer song	baking a gingerbread man
collar bell	tiny little bell
tinkle bell	ding bell

Loud Sounds

bells	fire engine bell
chimes	chuckwagon bell
supper bell in olden days	bicycle bell
train bell	two bottles hitting
jingle bell	horn
school bell	cow bell
storm	wake-up bell
church bell	police bell
ice cream bell	siren
store bell	football bell
rooster	telephone

Sounds When Held in Hand

hammer on a rock	water dripping
bottle on a rock	gold
two plates crashing together	rain
two sticks hitting	school alarm

THE SOUNDS OF HALLOWEEN

These are the sounds of Halloween as described by third graders
from three classes. When put together in story form and accompanied by
rhythm instruments, they make a very spooky story!

witch laughing	cat meowing	rapping
firecrackers	witch zooming	bells
cheering	sheets swishing	talking
ghost howling	feet on sidewalk	noises

Summary

A sound music program in the elementary school is one which frees children to use music in original ways. In order to accomplish this goal, certain skills must be developed creatively by a teacher who works closely with a music specialist. Both teachers should expose the children to many experiences which promote divergent thinking and acting, which are open-ended in nature and which result in self-satisfying, creative and exciting products. Continual exposure to open-ended experiences will re-enforce the fluency and quality of ideas from the children, so music learning truly makes a contribution to creative development.

TO THE COLLEGE STUDENT

1. Try to write some musical stories. Even if you cannot play a piano, you will find a great deal of satisfaction in creating a musical symbol for each character of the story to be played each time he appears. Tell your story to some children and watch their reaction.

2. Take an inventory of your class and find out who plays musical instruments. Have them bring them to class some day and experiment to find all the ways you can to teach the children creatively.

3. Jazz is truly one of the most creative of all music, especially in the jam session where music is made up spontaneously. Have a jam session with your colleagues and their instruments.

4. If you do not play an instrument, experiment with an auto-harp or flutophone or make some of the instruments mentioned in this chapter and create some music. Record it and evaluate it during the playback.

5. Discuss all the ways you can to teach the instruments of an orchestra to children, creatively.

6. Make a collection of good, children's musical recordings. Listen to some of them in class and discuss *many* ways they may be used with children. Some suggestions: "Peter and the Wolf," "Little

Indian Drum," "Hansel and Gretel," "The Littlest Angel," "A Walk Through the Forest" and others.

7. Make a list of all the ways that music may be tied in with other aspects of the elementary school program.

TO THE CLASSROOM TEACHER

1. Check your music program and note how it is tied in with the rest of the day. Do you allow your music teacher to handle *all* musical instruction? In what ways can you improve this situation?

2. Design a music center for your classroom and think of all the independent activities that could be provided for the children in this center, both before school and during lunch hour.

3. Think of all the ways you can to tie music into the teaching of a science unit on sound.

4. Encourage your children to set some of their original poems to music.

5. Find out what instruments the children in your classroom can play (anything from a mouth organ to a violin) and ask each child to bring his instrument to school and play it for the other children. Make up songs or stories to go with the music or about the instrument.

6. Ask the children to paint the sounds of each musical instrument brought into the room.

TO THE COLLEGE STUDENT AND THE CLASSROOM TEACHER

1. Help the children to collect all sorts of materials which will produce a sound and then synchronize these sounds into an orchestra or a sound story. (Example: rubber bands stretched over a cigar box, glass tubing of different lengths suspended from a door casing and tapped with a mallet or a spike, a cork pulled from a bottle, cellophane crackling, etc.).

2. List all the *creative* ways you can to introduce the reading of music to primary youngsters.

3. Through what creative means could you introduce key signatures and music symbols to young children?

4. Make up a story which has bongo drum accompaniment and tell it to some children. Then encourage them to create a story using only a marimba for accompaniment.

5. Ask the children to make a list of sounds they will hear on the Fourth of July and then try to find a rhythm instrument to depict the sound, for example: slapping two sticks together for an exploding firecracker, beating a drum for the parade, ringing bells for the waving of the flag, etc. Put these sounds together into a Fourth of July story.

6. After children write poems, encourage them to choose an appropriate recording to serve as a musical background when each reads his poem to the class.

7. Encourage the children to select music to serve as a background for their choral speaking exercises (see Book II, *Creative Teaching of the Language Arts in the Elementary School,* Chapter V).

SELECTED BIBLIOGRAPHY

COLEMAN, SATIS N. *Creative Music in the Home.* New York: John Day Company, 1939.

ELLISON, ALFRED. *Music With Children.* New York: McGraw-Hill Book Co., Inc., 1959.

HOOD, M. V. and E. J. SCHULTZ. *Learning Music Through Rhythm.* Boston: Ginn and Co., 1949.

HUGHES, LANGSTON. *The First Book of Rhythms.* New York: Franklin Watts, Inc., 1954.

LANDECK, BEATRICE. *Children and Music.* New York: William Sloane Associates, 1952.

MORGAN, HAZEL N. (ed.). *Music in American Education.* Chicago: Music Educator's National Conference, 1955.

MURSELL, JAMES. *Music and the Classroom Teacher.* Morristown: Silver Burdett Co., 1951.

MYERS, LOUISE K. *Teaching Children Music in the Elementary School.* Englewood Cliffs: Prentice-Hall, Inc., 1952.

NEW YORK STATE EDUCATION DEPARTMENT, Bureau of Elementary Curriculum Development. *Children the Music Makers.* Albany: The Bureau, 1953.

VI
Creative Teaching Through Rhythms and Dance

... Movement is the very essence of creative rhythmic expression. This form of creativity differs from all others because the body is the instrument of expression. Awareness of this sensitive instrument is one of the first steps in exploration in a rhythms program.[1]

GLADYS ANDREWS

TO THE READER

Do you have a modern dance group in your town or on your campus? Ask someone from this group to talk to your class, or, better yet, give a demonstration. Or, view the film Dance Your Own Way. *How does this type of dancing differ from classical dancing? Which of the two types best follows the principles of creativity (stated in Chapter I) and makes possible its development? Try your hand at giving a report to the class through the use of a dance.*

Introduction

A dance is movement put to a pattern. It is a form of expression and can be employed as a means of developing creativity. In an accepting, permissive atmosphere, the dance may be utilized to develop divergent thinking processes. Originality may be fostered, individuality can run rampant, and those characteristics and qualities of creative people may be encouraged in a legitimate manner. The dance also provides a way for expending excess physical energy and emotional tensions.

There are other reasons why the dance should play a more important part in the elementary school curriculum than it currently does. Dance has crept into our culture more than we realize. Children witness dancing every day on television, and now children dance at an earlier age than ever before. Dancing is an integral part of our musical shows such as *West Side Story* and *Oklahoma*. The dance portion of these productions has become so important that the

---

[1] Gladys Andrews, *Creative Rhythmic Movement for Children* (Englewood Cliffs: Prentice-Hall, Inc.), p. 26.

choreographer is given top billing with the producer. With the refinement of transportation and communication media, both rural and urban children are seeing more of these productions each year. Children are also exposed to classical dances such as ballet and those incorporated in opera. With such emphasis placed on the dance as a communicative device and as an aesthetic form, children need to know about it, to understand it and to use it for their own communicative and creative development.

Conditions Necessary for Creative Development through the Dance

In teaching creativity through the media of the dance, as through all the fine arts, certain conditions must be set.

Physical Conditions

The major material needed, of course, is space in which the children may experiment. Simple props may also be helpful. In the primary grades, soft, colorful scarves, ribbons and balloons encourage free expression through bodily movement. In the intermediate grades, other props usually found in the school environment may also serve as stimuli for dance expression; a football or basketball, a swing, roller skates, jump ropes and similar materials add a great challenge to the dance program. A good supply of recordings, a victrola, a piano, a drum or simple instruments which the children themselves can play are a necessary part of the program.

Ideally, a gymnasium is the best place to work out dances, but the movable seats in a classroom can be pushed out of the way so that the central space is available. On warm days, the lawn outside the school, or a flattened mound near the school, is ideal. In this instance, an old wind-up victrola is a valuable asset. The joy of using dance as a means of creative expression, however, lies in the fact that little or no equipment is really necessary except the children themselves.

Socio-emotional Conditions

A certain classroom atmosphere is essential if children are to feel free to express themselves through bodily movement. The "air of expectancy" mentioned so often in this set of books is of primary importance here.

Each child must feel he is an accepted part of a congenial group, so an atmosphere of permissiveness must exist in the classroom. Children must feel free to explore bodily movement without embarrassment. Creative interpretation can begin in the kindergarten, where children can be encouraged to create rhythms to which the teacher then creates music.

The dance program is closely allied to the music program; but in dance, movement and thought is of more importance than the music. Music accompanies and enriches the creative idea—it is not the dominant factor.

In one class, attempts were made to produce interpretive bodily movement without the use of a piano. Five and six-year-old children were encouraged to take off their shoes and stockings and to free themselves of inhibiting belts or sweaters in their clothing. They then sat in a circle on the floor. The teacher sat with them, and holding out her hands said, "Let's see all the things we can do with our hands!" All the children held out their hands and manipulated them in a variety of ways. Some spread their fingers, some wiggled them, some waved their hands through the air. One boy clapped. Then each child demonstrated what he could do with his hands, and the others imitated him. When clapping was introduced, the teacher asked if they could think of other noises they could make with their hands. Some ran their fingers rippling on the floor. Some spanked the floor, some snapped fingers, some beat a rhythm on the floor or other parts of their bodies. When the possibilities of hand movement were exhausted, they went through a similar experience with the use of the feet. Children wiggled their toes, bent their feet sideways, they stood and stamped, galloped, walked and ran. Each shared his idea with the others. The teacher next said, "I liked the sounds we made with our hands and feet. Let's take Bobby's sound for a minute and see what we can do with it. Now everyone listen while Bobby makes a sound with his hands."

Bobby proceeded to make a galloping sound with his fingertips on the floor. "I wonder what movements we can make up to go with Bobby's sound? Does anyone want to try while the rest of us make the sound?" Each child had an opportunity to interpret the sound in his own way. Some raced around the room, others galloped, some danced, some tipped their bodies from left to right and some just imitated others, as could be expected.

Eventually other sounds were introduced, both to accompany movement and to be interpreted by movement. Each child worked out a rhythm on the drum and the other children interpreted the rhythm with their bodies. The bell-like note of the triangle and the buzzing notes of the tambourine provided new experiences and new opportunities for interpretation. Finally, the piano was introduced to accompany some of the movements the children were making. After much experience with this, children interpreted some piano music.

A series of experiences of this kind, utilizing rhythmical noises rather than music, helps the child to concentrate on his own ideas and his own bodily interpretation. Children discover what they can do with their arms, their legs and their trunks. And they explore the possibilities of putting these movements into patterns.

Poise and fluent bodily movement can be developed in children who are not under constant pressure to conform to adult ideas. Much of the clumsiness which growing children exhibit is due to the restriction modern living places on their experimentation with changing bodily growth. The running, jumping, tree-climbing, swimming, leaping and tumbling of children are the natural ways they develop grace of movement. If our culture limits children in the pursuit of these activities, the school can help provide an artificial means for meeting these needs by continuing the experiences children can have in developing body motion in physical education and in dance experiences. The release of tension and pent-up bodily energy renders a therapeutic value to such experiences.

After the child has learned to interpret sound and music, and to create pattern and rhythm, he will enjoy learning dances which other people have created. In the primary grades, simple folk dances such as winding the May pole and song dances like "Brother Come and Dance With Me" are enjoyed by most children. Their own creative representation should not be dominated by traditional dance forms, however.

Children soon learn that a dance is merely movement put to a pattern. They will make up movement of their own with the music added later and they will also learn to interpret music with movement. Sometimes the two techniques can be combined, such as in a Mexican mask dance where a group pattern is followed, then during the dance one child at a time breaks away from the circle of dancers and develops his own individual interpretation of the music. Children in the intermediate grades enjoy folk dances. The Virginia Reel, square dancing and the minuet are each learned best by children who have had a wide background of experience in the creative interpretation of music.

One fifth grade, studying the Inca culture of Peru, came across some authentic ceremonial music of the Incas. They interpreted this music as they felt it would be danced and made costumes and props to go with their dance. Experiences such as this foster group initiative.

Group dancing starts in the early grades and becomes more important to the child as he develops, looking more and more to his peers for approval and prestige. By the time he reaches the intermediate grades this phase of his development is at its peak. This is the opportune time for teaching group dancing. Group interpretation through dance can be as creative as individual interpretation and can have as its product an experience in social cooperation and expression. Such group work can help provide a means for boys and girls of the intermediate grades to bridge the awkward gap between the sexes. This is the time when modern social dancing should be introduced.

A group of fifth and sixth grade girls worked on the interpretation of a dance. The two grades numbered off into five groups. A pianist played a selected piece of music and the groups listened. Each group then went off into different sections of the auditorium and discussed the music. Various members of the group tried different steps and movements to interpret the music. Frequently, a group returned to the piano and asked for the composition to be replayed, then they would go back and work out more ideas. A time limit had been set for this preliminary planning when the dance pattern was "roughed out." As soon as each group felt ready, the participants announced it to the teacher and seated themselves around the edge of the auditorium until all the groups were ready.

The teacher called on group one to give its interpretation. Each member took his place in the center of the circle and the pianist played while they presented their ideas. After the first attempt, the dance was evaluated. The audience picked out especially good points, indicated weak ones where the pattern was inclined to disintegrate or where the pattern was followed for too long a period or was too repetitious. The group went through it a second time with some changes and then seated themselves to watch the interpretation of the other groups. The procedure was repeated until each of the five groups had presented its ideas and had been evaluated. Then the groups again went to different sections of the gymnasium to work at refining and polishing their interpretations. After a period of time each group again presented its finished product. Often this was carried another step by inventing one dance from ideas presented by the various groups.

These experiences were, of course, preceded by discussions about what constitutes a dance. These children, who had many creative experiences during school, approached experiences such as this with enthusiasm. Often a different composition was played for each group and an interpretation was worked out by the same procedure as that presented above. Later on, these children worked in reverse, making up a dance pattern and then finding appropriate accompanying music.

A group of fifth and sixth grade boys worked with their music teacher and gymnasium teacher to create a football dance. The gymnasium teacher had taken them as a group to see a group of male dancers. This group, clad in shorts, assembled the dramatic movements of the football game into a pattern, while the music teacher and some of the students worked out piano music to accompany the patterns. The result was excellent team cooperation and a highly imaginative product.

The boys utilized the graceful movements of the run and the kick-off, the flowing sweep of the forward pass and the patterned movements of the line up. Comic relief provided contrast with exaggerated movements of the huddle and the touchdown. A great deal of individual interpretation was present in tumbling, falling and turning somersaults. So effective was this dance that it was given as an assembly program for both children and parents to enjoy.

The same group of combined fifth and sixth grade boys and girls created an Indian dance which was an interpretation of life in an Indian village. Peaceful music provided the mood for the opening of the dance where squaws, occupied in carrying out the many village activities to patterned movements, sat in a circle. One pounded corn, one wove a blanket, another sewed buckskin, and still another scraped a deer hide. Then the peace of the village was broken by a messager of the village bringing news that the braves were returning from war. The braves entered, full of the stories of their conquests which each told through motion. A war dance followed to celebrate the victory. The dance ended with the women calmly pursuing their tasks while the braves went off to the hunt as the day ended.

After many interesting experiences of this kind, where individual and group imagination has a chance to operate, children of this age often become interested in social dancing and ballet, acrobatic and ballroom dancing. This particular group learned to waltz, fox trot, conga, rhumba, jitterbug, stomp and twist. In the spring, they sponsored several dances to which children of other grades and parents were invited. The children planned the decorations, the programs, the invitations, the refreshments and the dance itself. A record player was used to supply the music. Proper social graces were studied and the children practiced techniques of introduction and proper social customs. Equipped with the knowledge of the correct thing to do in a given social situation and with the techniques for doing it, children obtain a great deal of security and poise in a social situation.

Psychological Conditions

In addition to the social security a child feels in being an accepted member of a congenial group and the joy of working in a permissive atmosphere, there are other psychological securities he needs to feel free to express his own creative ideas with his body. As we have seen from the above illustration, all suggestions for bodily interpretation must be accepted. No child should be made to feel that his contribution will be considered silly.

It should be understood that a creative dance is a new one, either created from original ideas of children or a combination of the dances or dance ideas they already know put into new patterns. At the onset of the experience, the product is unknown. This implies that all children should be encouraged to work through the creative process to a creative product. A highly-motivating force is necessary to accomplish this objective of involvement. Many ideas for inducing high-tension motivation are presented on the following pages.

Since aesthetic release must come with the finished product, the development of the dance should be success-oriented. Completed products need not be refined except in those instances where they are to be presented to other groups. Once again, in this instance, we utilize the principle of deferred judgment to develop creativity. In the refinement of the dance the principles of elaboration, alteration, expansion and others may be applied.

Intellectual Conditions

Aside from the high-tension motivational force which must be a challenge to the intelligence of the child, certain other intellectual conditions must be set. Children should understand the place of dance in the cultures of the world. In the intermediate grade program children can learn the dances of each country as part of their social studies units, in the social studies unit on *Mexico* described on page 28. Children should know what these dances do for and communicate to the people of a particular culture. They should also know that these dances are the classical dances of the country and as such, constitute part of the folklore of that country. By and large, the learning of these dances does not develop the creative powers in the children who learn them, but serve the purpose of showing them a multitude of ways that thoughts and feelings can be put into movement. From these movements they may create new patterns of movement. They should also understand that the success of performing any dance lies in learning it well so that all the dancer's movements are highly synchronized. This is a far cry from purely creative dances where they form their own ideas for movements into new patterns. The former develops the convergent thought processes, while the latter develops the divergent thought processes. The contrast of the two processes may be likened to two kinds of workbook exercises in reading, where one exercise instructs a child to draw something exactly like a given picture, while the other asks him to draw something he saw on the way to school.[2]

Creating a dance is a problem–solving process. The creative result is a pattern of movement, and both the process and the product can be creative. Performing an existing dance is a problem-solving process, but neither the process nor the product is creative. Both concentrate largely on imitation.

The Teacher's Role

The development of creative rhythms and creative dance lend themselves wholeheartedly to the principles of creative teaching described in Chapter I. As in all creative teaching, the role of the teacher in a dance program is to provide situations for all kinds of dancing. A good school program of this nature is one where the physical education teacher and the classroom teacher work closely together to develop a serious, developmental program, rather than a fragmented

[2] James A. Smith, *Setting Conditions for the Creative Teaching of Reading and Literature in the Elementary School* (Boston: Allyn and Bacon, Inc., 1967).

one where neither knows what the other is doing. Procedures used in the classroom and in the gymnasium must be closely related to the child's normal growth and development. The dance program, to accomplish its creative objectives, must be carefully planned and not confined to gym periods alone.

In assuming a team role for the development of creativity in children, the physical education teacher and the classroom teacher assume new responsibilities for the physical education program of boys and girls. Much of the militaristic, dogmatic teaching of physical education must be replaced by helping children understand how they may grow through creative activity. Through creative methods, the objectives of recreation, balanced living and mental hygiene are more directly accomplished than through current physical fitness programs. A recent book, *Physical Education for Today's Boys and Girls,* gives ample evidence as to how this might be accomplished.[3] It is a significant contribution to the area of creative teaching because it translates into action those conditions necessary to foster creativity in that area. A book with a fresh outlook, it buries the concept of those dull and stereotyped gym periods which place children in puppet roles, marching, drilling and playing games so highly organized that real goals are more often thwarted than met. On the grave of such a program blossoms the flowers of a new, creative and wonderful one. In this new program, our knowledge of boys and girls and how they grow and develop is really put to work. The dynamics of growth and development are brought together in a meaningful, comprehensive and clear-cut manner.

Robert S. Fleming, in an introduction to the book, states:

> The creative quality inherent in the teachers' work with children is clearly brought out. But neither physical education nor creativity is treated as an end in itself. The total process is conceived as a means of fostering the total growth of boys and girls . . .

The authors state: "When movement and growth are viewed together they provide a framework for physical education," and they proceed to list some basic beliefs about movement education. Among these are:

1. Movement can be an important factor in learning.
2. Movement experiences can stimulate thinking.

[3] Gladys Andrews, Jeanette Saurborn, and Elsa Schneider, *Physical Education for Today's Boys and Girls* (Boston: Allyn and Bacon, Inc., 1960).

3. Movement experiences can help children understand their own ideas and feelings.
4. Movement experiences can help children understand other people.
5. Movement can be a form of communication.
6. Movement can provide for self-expression.
7. Movement education can help children develop social interaction.
8. Movement education can help children develop physical skills in common and unique activities.
9. Movement education can provide opportunities for cooperation and competition.
10. Movement education can help children clarify concepts about their environment.[4]

The text which follows develops these objectives in a creative and exciting manner. A physical education program such as the one described in this book contributes to the creative development of children in every respect.

In creative teaching through the use of rhythms and dance, the teacher must build strong, positive tensions in children which will be released through expended physical energy. Once the children have become involved in this process, the teacher withdraws from her role and the children face the unknown. The teacher shifts her role from that of leader to that of a guiding support, helping the children develop their own ideas toward a solution to their own problems. Children are helped to think for themselves.

As often as possible, teachers will relate the teaching of dance to other areas of the curriculum. In the other books in this series, suggestions are made as to how dance might be related to each area of the curriculum. It is important, too, to remember that by using dance as a media of expression, creative qualities and powers may be developed in *individuals* as well as in *groups*. As in music, there must be a continual program of experiences in dancing which will serve as a stimuli and a background for movement interpretation and creation.

The teacher should provide many experiences in other areas of the school curriculum which can be translated into patterned movement. As in the other forms of creative expression, the subject matter in the dance is basically derived from current interests of the children. Almost any experience can be translated into a dance expression: a football game, a holiday, a trip to the zoo, a nursery rhyme, or a piece of popular music. If the subject appeals to teacher and pupils, it can be used.

[4] Ibid, preface by Robert S. Fleming.

FIGURE 6–1. *There are many dances to be danced, and many to be created.*

Developing Creativity Through the Use of Rhythms and Dance in the Primary Grades

A well-planned program for developing creativity through the use of rhythms and dance should result in more creative individuals, better-adjusted individuals, and individuals who possess greater aesthetic appreciation and enjoyment.

1. In the book, *Creative Rhythmic Movement for Children* by Gladys Andrews, many excellent suggestions are given for creative development through rhythmic expression. This text may serve as a guide in this area, since demonstration lessons are written up as illustrations for a rich and varied program in creative rhythms.[5]

[5] Gladys Andrews, *Creative Rhythmic Movement for Children* (Englewood Cliffs: Prentice-Hall, Inc.), pp. 41–43 and pp. 46–55.

2. To explore rhythmic movement with children, ask them to:

Make yourself round.
Make yourself as tall as possible.
Move only one part of your body.
Move every part of your body.
Make your body be as quiet as possible.
Reach as far as possible.
Be as short as you can . . . as tall.
Tremble like a leaf.
Chug like a train.
Slink like a cat.
Crawl like a snake.
Wiggle like a worm.
Walk like an elephant.
Gallop like a horse.
Be a grasshopper.
Be a rabbit.
Be a bear.
Walk like a spider.

3. At the beginning of children's school experience, the teacher can suggest that they dance the following patterns:

Their interpretation of musical recordings of many moods and tempos.
A happy dance.
A sad dance.
An angry dance.
A wild dance.
Dance like a rabbit, a duck or a cat.
Dance like an automobile, a bicycle or a train.
Dance the movements of nature: swaying trees, buzzing bees, falling snow, splashing rain, etc.
Play one musical instrument and make up a dance peculiar to it.
Make up rhythms or a dance showing work on the farm: the plowing, the cutting of the grain, etc.
Create a dance about men working on a railroad.
Dance a story about spooks and Halloween night.

More complex dance suggestions for upper primary grades are:

Dance a trip to the zoo, the circus, etc.
Dance a recess period using the movements of the playground equipment.
Plan a dance that tells about a day in a lumber camp, an Indian village, Disneyland, etc.

Put your favorite story to a dance dramatization.

Make up cowboy dances using props such as ropes, ten gallon hats, etc.

Make up dances about sailors and the sea.

4. Plan rhythms and dances which include all the following movements: bouncing, turning, twisting, swinging, hopping, walking, jumping, running, leaping, stretching, pulling, pushing, bending, shaking, trembling, whirling and squatting.

5. Select music which will help the children to explore tagging, catching, volleying, dribbling, batting, bouncing, skipping, chinning, galloping, sliding, kicking, throwing, whirling and doing a cartwheel.

6. Favorite poems and stories can be used to create rhythmic movement which can later be put to music and dance.

7. To establish relationships to space, have a child curl up in a large cardboard box with the top off so the rest of the children can notice body position in tight, cramped quarters. Discuss the way he feels released from the box into the classroom. Then discuss the way one feels when he enters a gymnasium free of furniture. Children can show movements to express this relationship to different *amounts* of space.

8. Action songs and movement songs give children opportunity to work out creative dance patterns. Many poems lend themselves to this sort of activity also, such as:

"The Duel," by Eugene Field
"The Sugar Plum Tree," by Eugene Field
"The Owl and the Pussycat," by Eugene Field
"Fog," by Carl Sandburg
"Wynkyn, Blynkn, and Nod," by Eugene Field
"The Elf and the Dormouse," by Oliver Herford

9. Children can tell stories of their own experiences, or the experiences of others, through dance. They can relive an airplane flight, an Easter egg hunt, a treasure hunt, or decorating the Christmas tree, through rhythms which may be worked into a dance pattern. Or they may enact Indian ceremonials, the westward movement, work in a factory, an ancient ritual or almost any other experience where their imaginations may be set free to interpret material they have read.

10. Playground equipment and gymnasium equipment such as balls, bats, sticks, hoops, jump ropes, hurdles, etc. can be explored to work out musical dramatizations. Rolling the ball down a line of chil-

dren, each of whom must jump over it, will create a rhythm to which music can be added. Throwing the ball from person to person creates another rhythm. Throwing the ball as high as possible creates still another. Soon children can find a variety of movements to dramatize and use in a pattern. They can explore music to accompany these movements or the teacher can create music to accompany their movements. Various bouncing, turning, clapping and catching patterns can be developed into new games or songs.

11. Cut small strips of paper and write directions, such as those given below, on each of two pieces. Fold many such papers and put them in a hat or box. All the childen then draw a paper and each reads his own but no one else's. The teacher calls on a child to stand and dramatize the idea on his paper. As soon as the other person from the pair recognizes the dramatization, he joins the first child. All the children try to guess what the two are doing. Depth is added to the experience if the teacher creates music to accompany the performing children.

Sample directions:

Be a ping pong ball in the middle of a game; be a top; be a monkey swinging from the trees; leap like a frog; swing like a pendulum; play a game of baseball; be a yo-yo; be a typewriter; be a scooter; walk a tight rope; be a bowl of jello; row a boat; be a steam shovel; be a Raggedy Ann doll; be an egg beater; be a penguin; be a submarine; be a tin soldier; grow like a flower.

After children have dramatized some of these simple movements, more complicated convergent thinking powers may be developed by the application of elaboration, modification or other creative ideation techniques mentioned in Chapter I. For instance, instead of the simple directions above, elaborations such as these may appear on the slips of paper:

Be a top with the wind blowing; be a frog jumping from lily pad to lily pad; swing like a pendulum in a grandfather's clock at midnight; be a yo-yo that breaks; be a scooter with a big boy riding it; walk a tight rope carrying three chairs; be an egg beater beating a thick batter of fruit cake; be a top with the snow falling around it; or be a top in the spring, in the mud or in the sunshine.

12. The children themselves can suggest various conditions under which a top functions and these could be translated into creative movement. Children can learn to tell simple, original stories through this technique, thereby expanding their creative power.

Miss Hart's third grade developed an exciting story about a boy who had a yo-yo with which he had a variety of adventures. First the yo-yo was new and went very well. Then it became old and worn and operated very uncertainly. Finally the string broke and it could no longer function at all. The boy bought a new string for the yo-yo and it was in topnotch operating condition again. One day the yo-yo became a hero when the boy dropped a quarter down a drain and the yo-yo retrieved it because the boy put his gum on the yo-yo and shot it down the drain. Everyone was happy about this and the boy and the yo-yo were never apart.

The dance movements which the children worked out were the movements of the yo-yo, not the boy. The challenge to their thinking in developing a new yo-yo, an old yo-yo, a broken yo-yo, a heroic yo-yo and a happy yo-yo was excellent, and the variety of rhythmic patterns they invented was remarkable.

13. A book by Paul and Anne Barlin called *Dance A Story* suggests many ideas and illustrations for teachers to use along this same line (produced by RCA Victor and distributed by Ginn and Co.).

14. Show the film *Marcel Marceau's Pantomimes* to the children for a study as to how the body may be used to communicate ideas (19 min., color, Brandon Films).

15. Take children to the playground, to a wooded area or a meadow near the school and have them explore the environment. Use the materials they find as an idea for a rhythm or dance, or as a part of it.

16. Miss Nichols's first grade made up a dance using sticks which they tapped, crossed and touched. Miss Smith's third graders watched ants making an anthill and then imitated the movements in a dramatization for which Miss Smith played some original music. Mr. Arnold's fourth grade watched the second graders on the playground and used their movements in climbing the jungle gym, swinging, teetering and riding the merry-go-round in making up a dance for the spring festival depicting school life.

17. When a child is reluctant to join the group, persuasive materials allow him to forget himself. Balls, balloons, scarves, hoops, his use of the drum to keep time with the group activity and his decision as to whom to give it to next all serve to remove inhibitions.

18. There are simple ways to improvise at the piano to accompany almost any song, or rhythmic activities. Those illustrated are in two keys, C, and F, with the three principle chords I, IV, and V^7 Musical Example 1.

Musical Example 1

These may be played in whatever rhythm desired, always coming home to I. An airplane may rise from low to high on the piano, and make a safe return. A train may chug along slowly, or be a fast express. Running, skipping, jumping, walking, stamping or tiptoeing may be equally well accompanied.

Some books give the teacher material for developing creative rhythms with children. One such book is, *Let's Dance a Story* by Katherine Mace (Abelard-Schuman, Ltd., New York, 1955).

Developing Creativity Through Use of the Dance in the Intermediate Grades

Intermediate grade children will respond to stimuli such as this:

1. Plan a dance that shows machinery working.

2. Plan ancient tribal dances.

3. Dance a street scene: children playing, women marketing, etc.

4. Make up a dance about a baseball game, basketball game, etc.

5. Show a meeting of the United Nations through a dance pattern.

6. Make up a dance around a meeting of the Olympic games.

7. Divide into small groups and have each group pantomime a street corner scene, a school cafeteria scene, a scene at the movies.

8. Dance a part of your favorite television show.

9. Put your favorite sidewalk games into a dance. Girls: hopscotch, jump rope, hide and seek; Boys: mumbledy-peg, run-sheep-run, snatch the hat, etc.

10. Learn dance rhythms peculiar to other countries and incorporate them into some creative dancing: Spanish, Japanese, etc.

11. Dramatize through dance the launching of an astronaut.

12. Have some children chant basketball and football cheers while others work out rhythms to go with them.

13. The drum can be effectively used, by the teacher who cannot play the piano, as an introduction to rhythm band playing. The drum can also be explored as an instrument capable of many communications itself.

Mr. Mack helped his sixth grade boys work up a drum rhythm to accompany an Inca dance of sacrifice. The various drum rhythms provided sole accompaniment for the dance.

14. Mathematical concepts can be shown through dance steps. A simple problem such as multiplying by twos can be used as a base for a gymnasium dance. While the class chants two times one is two, one couple skips around the room. At the change of the chant to two times two is four, they select another couple and the four of them do a new step. These four in turn choose four more and so on until the entire class is in action.

Other ideas may be utilized such as:

Ten ones equals one ten.
A straight line is the shortest distance between two points.
Dividing is a short way of subtracting.
Subtraction is easy.

15. Older boys will enjoy showing their strength and agility on ladders, horizontal bars, turning bars, chinning bars and gymnasium ropes.

16. Children in the intermediate grades enjoy charades. Have them work in groups to dance out a charade around any given topic (an industry, a school situation, a school problem, a recent out-of-school experience). They can select music to accompany their dramatization or create music with drums, piano, xylophone, mouth organ or any simple instrument, as they go along.

17. Some of the ideas suggested in Chapter VI, Book II, *Creative Teaching of the Language Arts in the Elementary School,* can be used for interpretation through rhythm or dance patterns:

1. Pretend you are your favorite dessert—dance it out (ice cream melting, fluffy desserts shown with light steps, fruit shown by shapes, etc.).

2. Dance how it feels to be sad, happy, ugly, silly.
3. Pretend you are your favorite toy and act it out through rhythms (Raggedy Ann, Ballerina, a steam shovel or a boat).

18. Children enjoy chants. Often choral speaking can be combined with rhythms to result in some interesting dance creations. Part of Mrs. Frederick's sixth grade chanted Sandburg's "Chicago," while the rest of the class danced to it with simple props. This occurred after a study of famous cities in the United States.

19. Listen to the things children say before school. Select a particular catchy phrase and have the children work it into a chant. Create a rhythm to go with the chant.

Mr. Elferd heard his children repeating a phrase, "Oh, knock it off!" before school. In the middle of the morning when he felt the children needed a break, he wrote this phrase on the chalkboard. He discussed what it meant, and then the children made a list of all the places where it would apply. The children then stood in a circle and while the children in the circle chanted the phrase using various tempos, other children put some of the situations to a rhythm in the center of the circle.

20. Some television commercial songs and chants can be used in this manner.

21. Children can chant poems and songs while classmates enact them through rhythms. Many kinds of chants can be used for this purpose, such as working poems, sea shanty poems, poems of the cowboys, Congo chants, spirituals, oriental chants and chants which use instruments such as paddles, sticks or bells.

When children in the intermediate grades have used their bodies to create various rhythmic patterns they will find it easy to sense the feelings and the story of the folk dances and popular dances of America. Some dances they will enjoy are square dances, the Virginia reel, the Schottische, the two-step, the Conga, the jig, the mazurka, the cha-cha, the fox trot, the Bunny Hop, the Lindy Hop, the stomp and the jitterbug.

Summary

Children are born in rhythm and movement. Music and bodily movement are part of the innate equipment which comes with each child—the most primitive and direct means which he has to express himself. Each child can be helped to develop creative communication with these innate skills providing, of course, that he has the privilege of being in a classroom where musical ability and expressive bodily movement are considered to be important and where conditions have been set to develop these skills through creative exploration of their growth.

TO THE COLLEGE STUDENT

1. Every dance the world has ever known is rooted in tradition. Divide your class into committees and have each committee investigate the origin of the folk and popular dances that appeal to you. Their reports will be more interesting if they can play appropriate music and demonstrate a part of each dance. After the reports are finished, discuss ways you could use this technique and this knowledge with children.

2. Here are some films you will enjoy seeing in class. They will add to your own knowledge and show some creative uses of music in the classroom:

Design to Music, 5 min., color (International Film Bureau).
Children's Concert, 42 min., bw. (Encyclopedia Brittanica).
Hearing the Orchestra, 13 min., bw. (McGraw-Hill).
The Symphony Orchestra, 14 min., bw. (Encyclopedia Brittanica).

3. In many musical hits the element of surprise is used to produce a very creative effect. In a production of *The Music Man,* for instance, the number, "Seventy-six Trombones" was produced without a single instrument on the stage. It stopped the show. In *The Sound of Music,* children were used to create the "Do-Re-Me" number and it also stopped the show. Think of techniques you have seen in the theater which you felt were very creative. What made them creative?

4. From good modern musicals, select songs which might well be incorporated into a music program in the school. "Do-Re-Me" from *Sound of Music* is one, "A Hundred Million Miracles" from *Flower Drum Song,* is another. Think of others and the ways you could use them in the music curriculum.

TO THE CLASSROOM TEACHER

1. Look for good musical shows for children on television and assign one for listening pleasure. The day after the show discuss it with your children and try to analyze their music values and standards through the discussion.

2. Try using music and dance in relation to all the other subjects in the curriculum for a week. Use listening, singing, choral speaking and direct instruction:

    1. as a motivator.
    2. for background accompaniment.
    3. for relaxation.
    4. as a correlation with some subject.
    5. as a summary to a specific teaching situation.

3. Ask a group of children to plan to give a social studies report through the media of the dance rather than with words.

4. Assess the talent in your room by having a Friday afternoon talent show or concert. Find out who plays a musical instrument, who can dance and sing. The children who do none of these well enough to want to appear can work together to create songs, skits or a dance to present for their part of the show.

TO THE COLLEGE STUDENT
AND THE CLASSROOM TEACHER

1. Make a list of all the ways you can think of to help children create songs.

2. Learn to play a simple musical instrument such as a mouth organ, a flutophone, an autoharp or a marimba. Learn it by exploring the instrument and picking out simple tunes or creating tunes of your own. When you are comfortable with the instrument get help with some specific skills. Do you think children would like this approach? Is it more motivating than using practice pieces?

3. Tell a nursery rhyme, children's story or your own story, using the piano to make accompanying sounds. Use low notes for animals, high notes for rain, etc. You will be amazed at how the piano can help, even if you have had very little or no training. Try to

create some musical stories. Tell them to children and note their reactions.

4. Discuss all the ways you can think of that you could effectively use a music consultant in a team teaching situation to enrich your daily program. Do the same with a physical education consultant.

5. Compile a file of recordings for various purposes: dramatization, rhythms, folk dancing, creative interpretation, music appreciation, etc. Contact your local music store for resources.

6. There is an enjoyable film about helping children to dance freely which you will want to see. Send for it at: California University, Los Angeles, California, 1958. (*Dance Your Own Way*, 10 min. col.)

7. Part of one other film shows some excellent techniques for developing creativity through the use of rhythms and dance. It would be worthwhile to see *Report In Primary Colors* (40 min., color). (The Maury School, Richmond, Virginia).

SELECTED BIBLIOGRAPHY

ANDREWS, GLADYS. *Creative Rhythmic Movement for Children.* Englewood Cliffs: Prentice-Hall, Inc., 1954.

ANDREWS, GLADYS. Jeanette Saurborn, and Elsa Schneider. *Physical Education for Today's Boys and Girls.* Boston: Allyn and Bacon, Inc., 1960.

COLEMAN, SATIS N. *Creative Music in the Home.* New York: John Day Co., 1939.

EASTMAN, MARCIA. *Creative Dance for Children.* Meredith: Mettler Studios, 1954.

HARTLEY, RUTH E., LAWRENCE K. FRANK and ROBERT M. GOLDENSON. *Understanding Children's Play.* New York: Columbia University Press, 1952.

HOOD, M. V. and E. J. SCHULTZ. *Learning Music Through Rhythm.* Boston: Ginn and Co., 1949.

HUGHES, LANGSTON. *The First Book of Rhythms.* New York: Franklin Watts, Inc., 1954.

LATCHAW, MARJORIE and JEAN PYATT. *Dance for Children.* Englewood Cliffs: Prentice-Hall, Inc., 1958.

MORGAN, E. and H. GRUBBS. "An Approach to Rhythms for Children," *Childhood Education*, XXIX (April, 1953), 383–7.

MURRAY, RUTH. *Dance in Elementary Education.* New York: Harper & Row, Publishers, Inc., 1953.

SHEEHY, EMMA D. *Children Discover Music and Dance.* New York: Holt, Rinehart and Winston, Inc., 1959.

Creative Teaching Through Dramatization

All the world's a stage.

SHAKESPEARE

TO THE READER

As you read the following chapter, think of the ways the techniques described therein could be used in a college or adult class on dramatics. Is there any part of Mr. Randall's lesson that would not serve as a motivator for creative development in such a class? Think of all the ways you can to use a dramatization in your class as a teaching device for the coming week. The ideas in this chapter will help you.

Introduction

Mr. Randall's fourth grade was busy with creative dramatics the afternoon I came to visit. Because Mr. Randall often used dramatics to develop creative expression, the children were eager with anticipation. "Mr. Randall," one of them told me, "always has something up his sleeve."

As the afternoon progressed, I could see that he did, indeed, have something up his sleeve.

"I am going to pass out slips of paper this afternoon," he said, "with something written on each paper. Do not show your papers to each other. Think of how you can show the class what is on your paper without speaking—by acting it out. We will all guess what you are trying to show us. Now, one other thing, two of you will have the same thing written on your slip of paper. The first one to act it out may be joined by the person who has the other slip of paper and he will show us how he planned to act it out. Then we will all guess what he is doing."

The folded strips of paper were distributed and read. Gasps. Squeals of delight. Giggles and guffaws. Chattering. "Gosh, how can I do that?"

I walked around the room and glanced at the papers.

> Be an egg beater.
> Be a watermelon seed.
> Be an astronaut.
> Be a guppy.
> Be a flat tire.
> Act like a scarecrow.
> Act like a paper of matches.

"Who is ready?" asked Mr. Randall.

Bill raised his hand.

"O.K., Bill, let's go!"

Bill went to the center of the room, smiling a secretive smile. He flopped down on the floor and curled himself into a tight ball hugging his legs close to his body with his arms clasped around them and his head buried in his knees. Finally he pressed his sneakers against the floor and with a vigorous thrust pushed himself across the shiny linoleum.

"Gee, I don't know what that is."

"What *is* he supposed to be?"

"Do it again, Bill."

He did it again. More discussion. Finally, from Gerald, "Ah, I got it!" He joined Bill. "It's on my paper, too," he said.

"Do you plan to dramatize it another way?" asked Mr. Randall.

"Uh-huh," said Gerald.

He pretended to hold something in both hands which he raised to his mouth. Then he took an enormous bite and chewed while he wiped his mouth with one hand, looked puzzled and spat vigorously.

"Very good," encouraged Mr. Randall.

"He's eating a watermelon," said Amy.

"Getting warm," said Bill, "but that's not what's on the paper."

"Think of Bill's actions now and you will get closer to it," advised Mr. Randall.

Suddenly Becky shouted, "A watermelon seed!"

Laughter and congratulations. "Boy, that was good!" "Who's next?" asked Mr. Randall.

Marie went to the middle of the room. She stood still for a minute then she bent her arms in a half circle from her sides. All at once she began flailing her arms and legs back and forth, crisscrossing them and turning her head from side to side.

"Who has a slip like Marie's—can you tell?" asked Mr. Randall.

"I do," said Phil, "and I was going to act it out the same way."

"All right—you do it with Marie. Try it once more and we will all guess."

Phil joined Marie. In a minute Pam said, "I know—are they eggbeaters?"

"Right," said Marie.

Other children dramatized their cards. The astronaut sat on the floor and fussed and fussed with make-believe adjustments. Then little by little he rose to his haunches, raised himself an inch at a time and finally thrust himself with a leap into the air.

The guppy went around the circle with his arms bent backwards to resemble fins while making his circular mouth open and close continually.

The flat tire made himself round and rolled a short way, then slowly unwound and lay flat on the floor.

The scarecrow stood limp and droopy and occasionally raised one limp arm to swat at something. When one child guessed it might be a scarecrow, she demanded an explanation for the swat.

"Just swatting the crows," the scarecrow answered.

The paper of matches held five fingers in the air and placed five more behind them. She then tucked the ten fingers under her chin. With a jerk she lifted her chin. One finger fell apart from the others. It was bent and made a sweeping motion as if it were being rubbed over the sandpaper on the match carton, and then applied to a fictitious cigarette in the actor's mouth.

And so a half hour went by faster than I could imagine. When everyone had taken part, the children asked, "Can we do more?"

"Well, I have some other things I think you might enjoy," said Mr. Randall. "I have here five pictures mounted on cardboard. Jimmy and Ethel, will you place them along the chalk board and while they are doing that I am going to ask the rest of you to count off by fives."

No sooner said than done. The pictures were of a comic nature, collected by Mr. Randall from the back page of Life magazine and from advertisements. One in particular depicted a little girl dressed in her mother's clothes, complete with high heels, gloves and an enormous hat, sitting on a curbstone crying her heart out. Before her in the road was a crushed doll carriage with the doll broken. Another showed a child looking with awe at his messy hands which were covered with fingerpaint up to the elbows.

"I am going to ask group one to take picture one, go to the back corner of the room in a buzz group and plan to dramatize the scene that happened before this picture was taken. You will stop the dramatization with the same pose as you see in the picture. It will be all action and no speaking. If you need more people for your presentation you may swap among the groups. I shall give you five minutes to prepare your play."

The children went to work at once and the results were imaginative, clever and delightful. After the presentations there was an evaluation of each skit with emphasis placed on the good parts of each and suggestions offered for other ways of doing them.

"I have something here which is quite difficult but you are clever and I am anxious to see what you will come up with," said Mr. Randall. "For these next skits I am going to ask for volunteers."

Mr. Randall unrolled three large sheets of paper and taped them to the chalk board. On the first one was a blue square cut from construction paper. On the second one were two tall, thin yellow strips of construction paper. On the third was a free form red glob of construction paper which resembled a wobbly ball.

"Now," said Mr. Randall, "what ideas do these give you? If you have an idea, take one, choose some of your friends to help you dramatize it and then we will guess which one you are dramatizing."

Elfreda volunteered first. She chose Marilyn and Gladys to help her. They went into a huddle in the corner and then took the center of the circle. Marilyn and Gladys stood far apart and Elfreda stood between them. Soon Gladys made a pushing motion with her hands. Elfreda drew up her face to resemble extreme pain and began to rotate and twist her body toward Gladys. Gladys in turn made a pushing motion with her hands and Elfreda rotated and twisted back toward Marilyn. This went on for a few minutes and then the girls stopped.

"Can you guess?" asked Elfreda.

"I think you are doing the red one," said Jimmy.

"That's right, but what are we?" asked Elfreda.

Many suggestions but no one guessed it. "I am a red balloon being batted back and forth who doesn't want to be batted back and forth," said Elfreda.

Jimmy, Gerry, Kevin and Al were next. They marched into the circle in military order. Jimmy and Gerry marched to one side of the circle, Kevin and Al to the other. They stood facing each other. Jimmy and Gerry cowered, looked worried, made pleading motions with their hands and finally hugged each other in fear. Kevin and Al snapped to attention, raised imaginary rifles to their shoulders, pointed at Jimmy and Gerry and fired. They were interpreting the two tall yellow strips of paper: two "yellow" (cowardly) soldiers facing a firing squad.

Debby and Marlene were the next volunteers. They faced each other and held hands. Both twisted their faces into cry-baby faces. Their shoulders shook with imaginary sobs. In this position they took two steps forward, two steps to the left, two steps backward and two steps to the right depicting a hollow square. They were the blue (sad) square.

Other interpretations of the abstract designs were given. Mr. Randall complimented the children. "Now for part of a story," he said.

The children had read *The Adventures of Tom Sawyer*. Now Mr. Randall chose the whitewashing scene and reread it. He divided the class into three groups and allowed them to meet in the various parts of the room to plan an interpretation of the scene with simple props. Each group then gave its interpretation to the rest of the class. At the end of each presentation the children told what they liked about each dramatization and made suggestions for succeeding groups, after which the entire afternoon was evaluated and the learnings summarized.

*   *   *

I chose this demonstration in Mr. Randall's room as an excellent illustration of the way that creativity can be developed through dramatization. So often dramatization is used as a garnish or embellishment to a lesson but in this instance it was a technique which was basic in accomplishing Mr. Randall's objectives. It is also an excellent example of creative teaching. It shows very dramatically how the principles of creative teaching mentioned in Chapter I can be applied in a classroom situation to develop creative power.

An overview of the plan of dramatization in the total elementary school curriculum was given in Chapter II. On the following pages are suggestions for the use of various kinds of play and dramatic situations which the author has seen used successfully in classrooms. They have impressed him because of their high-motivating power and because of the unusual, original and creative dramatizations which resulted from their use.

Situations Which Set Conditions for
Dramatic Play in the Primary Grades

Much of the dramatic play in the primary grades should be natural. In the classroom, children should be granted free time and the necessary environment to act out situations which are important to them. On the playground this is also true; equipment should be available which makes possible a great deal of dramatic play. Simple and unusual things can keep children highly motivated and give them an opportunity to identify with a variety of roles. An old automobile, stripped of all projections which may cause harm, affords endless opportunities for children to pretend they are Daddy: a school bus driver, a taxi driver and an airplane pilot. A large sewer pipe, firmly anchored so that it will not roll, can be a tunnel, a bridge or a hiding place. Every playground should have a gate on which children can swing. An old piece of railroad track gives them the chance to walk on it and provides practice in balancing. Slices of a tree imbedded in the ground serve as stepping stones, islands, and part of a Marine obstacle course. An old bath tub, partly sunk into the ground can provide a legitimate place for water play, for sailing boats or for blowing bubbles. A large sand box is a must, for all kinds of imaginative play can take place in it, even with a minimum amount of equipment. A tire swing or two gives a safe outlet for twisting and twirling and playing the circus acrobat. There should be a flat, surfaced area for games like hopscotch and for driving tricycles and trucks. A pair of stairs built up to a fenced-in platform can be a tree house, a theater balcony or a hill to climb. A small house or shed can become a hideout for cowboys, a club room or a miniature home.

All the usual commercially available playground equipment can contribute to dramatic play both in and out of doors, especially that equipment as produced by Creative Playthings which is safe, strong and not too detailed. Play equipment, like toys, will be limited in its use when it is too detailed. A toy bus painted to look like a real one is generally only a toy bus, but a block of wood with wheels can become a bus, a moving van, a truck, an automobile, an army transport, a tractor trailer, or a house trailer. The imagination of the child supplies the details and he will adapt it to his needs in a split second.

The first requisite to encouraging dramatic play is in settir conditions through the proper environmental equipment and climate both in and out of school. Children show their love for dramatization by carrying on long conversations with imaginary characters. Play is a necessary part of their developmental growth and in it they play many roles and use empathy to sense a variety of feelings. They also find outlet for their own emotions in doll or puppet play. They sometimes resort to bragging, telling tall tales, exaggeration and "squealing" on one another. So realistic is their play that they often find it difficult to differentiate between the real and the make-believe. This make-believe function of children's thinking is not lying, as many teachers believe, but it is imagination in full bloom—a basis for divergent thinking and creative production. It has been stilted in the past by teachers who insist that children tell only the real truth. Teachers need not be alarmed over the tall tales children tell or their

FIGURE 7–1. *Knighthood is a serious business for sixth graders who write their own play, make their own costumes and paint their own scenery.*

inability to differentiate between the impact of make-believe and the impact of reality. They should be accepting of both and help the child keep the two separated simply by commenting, "Billy told us a good make-believe story today and Mary told us a real one." Both should find accepting listeners for make-believe is the stuff from which creativity develops.

Common Situations Which Foster Dramatic Play

Use playground and schoolroom equipment.

1. Be an animal you saw on the way to school or on our science trip.

2. Imitate the postman, the mailman, the doctor, the nurse or an airline stewardess.

3. Play at shopping at the supermarket.

4. Dramatize the bus trip to school.

5. Play games which require dramatic interpretation, such as "Squirrel in the Tree," "Where From?" and "Catch the Rabbit."

6. Sing songs which require action and dramatic interpretation such as "Go In and Out the Windows," "John Brown's Baby," etc.

7. Use action songs and dances to develop dramatic expression such as "The Hokey Pokey," "The Bunny Hop," "Itsy-Bitsy Spider" and others.

8. Dramatize light things: air, marshmallows, Kleenex, feathers, dust or dandelion seeds.

9. Dramatize heavy things: bulldozers, iron, mud or stones.

10. Dramatize moving things: a train, a plane, a wheelbarrow or a lawnmower.

11. Dramatize quiet things: a statue, a rabbit or a librarian.

12. Dramatize fast things: a snake, a race car, a train, a plane or a waterfall.

13. Dramatize slow things: a turtle, an alligator, an old man or a worm.

14. Dramatize noisy things: an eggbeater, a lawnmower, a riveting machine or a motorboat.

15. Play *statues,* where one child twirls another by holding his arm, whirling him around and then releasing him. The twirled child freezes into the position in which he falls and all the children guess what he looks like.

*Situations Which Set Conditions for the
Development of Creativity Through the Use
of Dramatics in the Primary Grades*

1. Dramatize stories such as "The Little Rabbit Who Wanted Red Wings."

2. Dramatize poems and nursery rhymes such as "Jack Be Nimble," "Simple Simon" and "The Elf and the Dormouse."

3. Prepare for a trip to an unfamiliar place, such as a trip to the circus or the theater, by acting out the situation before you go. Buy tickets, learn how to enter the theater, etc.

4. Use a painting someone in the class has made and act out a story.

5. Do the same with an interesting magazine cover, advertisement or famous painting.

6. Dramatize the great current events of the day: the launching of a rocket, the flight of an astronaut or the launching of a ship.

7. Teach social courtesies through dramatizations: the manner by which people are introduced, the proper way to answer the telephone, to answer the door or to thank a hostess.

8. Dramatize the proper way to take a message to the office, to visit the school, to behave on a school bus, etc.

9. Invite older children to come into the classroom to present plays which are within the comprehension of the young children.

10. Take the children to school assemblies which are within their scope of understanding.

11. Use shadow plays, puppetry, magnetic puppet plays and other forms of dramatization as variation to your program. (See Book II Chapter V.)

12. Pantomime animals, people and objects and have the class guess what you are trying to be.

13. Develop dramatic skill by games, such as the following:

    a. Make yourself as small as possible, as tall as possible and as round as possible.

    b. Make yourself as quiet as possible, as noisy.

    c. Show me surprise, happiness, sadness.

    d. Pretend you are seeing your new baby sister for the first time.

14. Use fingerplay for quiet dramatics—especially ones the children have created. (See Book II.)

15. Create musical plays such as those described on page 105.

16. Dramatize the sounds of the various instruments of the orchestra.

17. Dramatize telephone conversations as they are described in Book II.

Situations Which Set Conditions for Creative Development Through Dramatic Play in the Intermediate Grades

1. Imitate instances from life around you such as:

    a. a pitcher warming up to throw a ball.
    b. a football player delivering a forward pass.
    c. a girl applying makeup.
    d. father shaving.
    e. little brother throwing a tantrum.
    f. older sister setting her hair.
    g. a man constructing a bookcase.

2. Play dramatic games such as *charades* and *statues*.

3. Make up stories and act them out to music similar to the musical story on page 105.

4. Dramatize favorite poems, songs and stories.

5. Play "Follow the Leader," where each child takes a turn at dramatizing and the rest follow. This idea may be built around themes such as a trip to the zoo, one child dramatizing a lion, the next a monkey and so on. Or a circus may be the theme, with one child being a clown, another a hawker, another a trapeze artist, etc.

6. Just as different emotions can be communicated through dramatization, so can different qualities. Ask children to think of an egg and then to be a fried egg, a hard-boiled egg, a poached egg, a raw egg and a scrambled egg.

7. Dramatize the qualities of inanimate objects: be a marshmallow, a piece of lead, glue, an eraser, a blotter, a thumb tack, a rubber band, a steam roller, a musical note.

8. Go through the actions of a particular player in a particular sport and have the class guess what you are playing.

9. Pretend you are a cave man or a prehistoric man with little or no verbal communication and ask groups in the classroom to show how a caveman might have communicated his idea. Some examples:

a. A certain caveman is ill with a raging fever. He wants water badly but is too ill to get it. Dramatize how he would let his peers know of his plight.

b. Two prehistoric men meet in the forest and try to tell each other about themselves: where they live, the size of their families, their ages, etc.

10. Pretend you are in a foreign land and cannot speak the language. Go marketing and try to buy groceries from a native.

11. Mr. Nellis asked the children to collect slang expressions and colloquialisms which could be dramatized literally and these were incorporated into comic dramatizations where one person read the story while a group acted it out. Some of the more clever ideas were:

a. *he ground his teeth.* At this point the actor took chalk from his mouth, put it in a meat grinder on the stage and proceeded to grind his teeth.

b. *the sun set.* The boy playing the part of the son sat down.

c. *drop dead.* The character collapsed.

d. *he made a B-line to the door.* The actor took a stack of cards from his pocket on which he had painted B's and laid them on the floor in a line to the door.

e. *he was always on the go.* The actor jumped on a traffic light.

f. *she was cutting up.* The actress chopped newspapers with a pair of scissors.

12. Role-playing, as mentioned in Chapter II, is a legitimate way for middle graders to become involved in free dramatic play. Many ideas for role playing are offered in Book V, *Creative Teaching of the Social Studies in the Elementary School,* Chapter IX. Some role and reverse-role playing situations may be built around instances like:

a. the breaking of a school rule and what might be done about it.

b. settling a playground fight or a classroom argument.
c. choosing an idea from many ideas for a theme for a classroom party.

Situations Which Set Conditions for the Development of Creativity Through Dramatics in the Intermediate Grades

If children have had their dramatic abilities stifled and are awkward
or embarrassed in expressing themselves through bodily movement
before the class, the teacher may regenerate this creative ability by
setting the proper social climate to free children to explore the
creative use of their bodies. Mrs. McCarthy, for example, spent a
little time each day on dramatics until the proper free climate was
established.

On the first day of her work with the children she gave each a
slip of paper on which she had written a direction. Each child acted
out this direction and the class guessed what it was. Some of the slips
read as follows:

1. Be an Indian stalking a deer.
2. Pretend you are a cowboy setting up camp.
3. Act like the nurse to a wounded soldier.
4. Be Dr. Kildare.
5. Imitate a woman shopping at a bargain basement.
6. Pretend you are a cow chewing her cud.

No evaluation was given at the end of the dramatizations because Mrs. McCarthy wanted the children to be completely comfortable with themselves.

The next day they were to imitate a favorite character from
literature, television or their acquaintances (providing every one in
the class knew this person, of course). For those who could not think
of a character, Mrs. McCarthy had put slips of paper with names
written on them in a box on her desk so that the children could
choose one. The next day there were excellent interpretations of
Sherlock Holmes, Davy Crockett, Daniel Boone, Amelia Earhart, Dr.
Kildare, Lucille Ball, the Adams Family from the television show,
Frankenstein, Allen Shephard, Sammy Davis, Louis Armstrong, the
First Lady, Florence Nightingale, Heidi and others.

On the following day Mrs. McCarthy began to work on the skills of dramatization by having the children choose characters whose portrayal called for unique interpretations and special actions. She prepared slips from which the children chose, asked them to observe such a situation or such a character at home or on the streets and then to dramatize it the next day. Some of these slips read as follows:

1. Be an old man.
2. Be a shy boy.
3. Imitate a cat catching a mouse.
4. Imitate a cat lapping up milk.
5. Cry like a little baby.
6. Sit down like an old lady.
7. Run like a four-year-old.
8. Walk like a Marine.
9. Be a tight-rope-walker.
10. Drink like a chicken.

After the dramatizations, the children were encouraged to evaluate each interpretation.

After a few periods of this work, Mrs. McCarthy held a discussion with the children and asked them how many expected to go to town with their parents over the weekend. Several planned to do so. She asked them to watch a particular person or scene on the street which appealed to them and to be prepared to dramatize it on Monday morning in pantomime so that the rest of the class might guess what each saw.

I was present in Mrs. McCarthy's room on that Monday morning and spent a delightful half hour watching the children act out their skits. Five girls dramatized a mother taking a group picture at a Sunday family picnic. One was a little child who wouldn't stand still. Of course, the inevitable happened as he turned his head just as mother clicked the shutter.

Four boys showed how their powers of observation were sharpened when they presented their scene. They stood in various slouching poses, leaning against the doorway, hands in pockets, bored expressions, listless actions. One tossed a coin, another twirled a watch, one scratched the ground with his toe. Suddenly they all became electrified. All eyes turned to one direction, bodies tensed, hats were shoved back on foreheads, eyes popped. All eyes and heads turned to the left and slowly swept to the right. Each boy stopped at least once in this process and let his eyes fall from eye level to the floor and up again. When all eyes and heads were finally as far to the right as possible the boys all joined in one unanimous wolf whistle. They had observed a group of sailors loitering on a street corner when a pretty girl passed by.

Other dramatizations were equally imaginative and challenging. One girl imitated a boy scout helping an old lady across the road, and another imitated a Sunday school teacher trying to quiet her brood.

I visited Mrs. McCarthy's room many times after that. She added voices to the dramatizations as her next step, rendering them superior in every way. Many of the children were writing their own plays. Several of the suggestions on the following pages are ideas I saw being employed by this truly creative teacher.

One day a lively discussion was in progress. The children had been assigned, as homework the previous day, to watch Marcelle Marceau, the great French pantomimist, on television. They were delighted with what they had seen and many times during the discussion a child would leap to his feet and imitate the great artist with no inhibitions at all. Mrs. McCarthy had changed this group from a shy, inhibited, self-conscious one to one where they could use their own bodies to communicate creatively.

Open-ended stories provide excellent situations for creative dramatizations. The teacher reads the beginning of a story and the children are divided in groups, each group dramatizing a possible ending. One such story, which Mrs. McCarthy wrote and read to her class, went like this:

THE DAY OF THE CIRCUS

The circus was coming! John read the posters over and over again! He had never been to a circus and the pictures fascinated him! He studied each one carefully and dreamed many dreams of the great day when each picture would become a reality.

From the time he saw the first poster outside the post office the day he went to town with his father, John knew he must go to the circus! He just had to see the animals depicted on the posters, and the beautiful ladies and handsome men. He doubted that these beautiful people could really fly through the air as they did in the posters, fight wild animals, or leap through fire while riding a horse as the posters showed them. He had to go—he must see for himself!

The posters said plainly that the admission price for children was one dollar and fifty cents. Where could he get so much money? His allowance was twenty-five cents a week and the circus was only two weeks away. That left a whole dollar for him to earn.

John talked to his mother about this. His mother had been in the hospital and his older sister was in college so money was pretty scarce. So John's mother could not promise him they could go to the circus. But he had to go—he just had to! So John began to look for ways he could earn money.

First he went to see Mr. Banks, the man who ran the corner store. Mr. Banks let John run errands after school. He figured he could earn a dollar easily this way. But, while working at the store, he heard all about the wonders of the circus which the posters didn't show: the pink lemonade, the cotton candy and the frozen custard. He also heard about the side shows with the bearded lady, the fat lady, the human skeleton and the sword swallower. John knew that he must partake of all these wonderful experiences too and that one dollar would not be enough. He must have more money—more!

So he mowed lawns on Saturday, sold lemonade at the roadside and helped a friend deliver papers on his newspaper route.

The day before the circus he had five dollars—five whole dollars to spend on all the things he wanted to try!

At last the day of the circus came. John was up bright and early. His father had promised to get him to town early so that he could see the circus unload at the railroad station and set up in Mr. Johnson's pasture where the show was to be held. John thought he would burst with excitement!

Father was ready at five o'clock. He hitched the horses to the wagon and John climbed into the high seat beside his father. Mother came to the door to wave goodbye. They arrived in town just as the train was pulling into the station. John could hardly wait to get out of the wagon and watch until father had disappeared up the road toward home. He fairly fell over himself trying to get to the front of the crowd. And sure enough—there were men already selling balloons and cotton candy. John decided he must try some. He put his hand into his pocket to get the fifteen cents to pay the man and made a sickening discovery. In his excitement he had left his wallet containing his five dollars on the bureau in his bedroom and father was already out of sight.

The five groups of children who dramatized endings to this situation each presented a different conclusion. Such experiences can be made doubly creative when children are encouraged to write open-ended stories themselves for the rest of the class to finish.

Use open-ended stories for children to dramatize. Some of these stories may be enacted by the class through some simple planning at the beginning and then left to role-playing and to free dramatics for the conclusion. Some suggestions follow:

1. You are in an airplane flying over the Amazon jungle and you develop plane trouble. Your pilot informs you that he must land.

He finds an opening in the jungle and brings the plane down. Although the passengers are shaken up, no one is seriously hurt. The plane, however, is damaged to the degree that you must get mechanical help. After you check to see that all the passengers are safe, everyone decides to start out on foot to the river, hoping to hail boats which might take you back to civilization. After consulting your pilot's compass and map, and estimating the direction of the river, the party starts out. As you approach the trees someone shouts, "Look." From the jungle a horde of natives emerge, dressed scantily and decorated with paint. They all carry spears and stand glaring at you.

Dramatize the scene up to this point and then continue to show how you would make friends with the natives, tell them of your plight, solicit their aid and reach your destination.

2. Quiz shows offer a fine opportunity for creative dramatic expression. "Celebrity Time" means that the children assume the qualities of certain famous characters that they know and represent them through speech and mannerisms on a mock quiz show. These quiz shows may be built around geography, history or science and can serve the dual purpose of developing creativity while checking on children's knowledge.

3. Surprise dramatizations offer an opportunity to set conditions for some creative writing or creative dramatics. In the middle of a writing class in a fifth grade, the door opened, a boy ran into the room and shouted, "Stop him, he's going to hurt me!" and rushed out. This event had been planned previously by the teacher and some children. The astonished children were then told it was a plot but to write how they felt or what they thought was happening. A more detailed instance might result in having the children dramatize the conclusion of the incident.

4. Social courtesies and proper behavior at social functions lend themselves well to dramatization. Miss Jarmon borrowed a telephone set from the telephone company and showed how the dial system works. After the children had studied this apparatus for a science lesson, Miss Jarmon posed several situations for which the telephone would be used. The children dramatized the situation by actually dialing the number and talking over the telephone. Telephone courtesy and the ways to handle various situations were discussed after each dramatization.

Other instances which lend themselves well to dramatization are:

1. Introductions: a child to an adult, a girl to a boy, a man to a man or a woman to a woman.
2. The proper way to ask a girl for a dance and the proper way to thank her when the dance is over.
3. Mannerisms of being a host or hostess.
4. The proper way to set a table.
5. The manner in which a hostess or host is thanked for a party.

Telephone dramatizations can also be used to help children find out some of the things they really want to know and that the teacher cannot tell them. For instance, after play-acting on the telephone had established accepted telephone courtesy, Mr. Readling had an extension telephone installed in his classroom and the children made lists of questions they might legitimately ask of an authority over the telephone. Then the children used their knowledge to make calls from which they gathered information to use in creative production. Some of their questions centered around the following topics:

The weather for the day, from the local weather bureau at the airport.

City census figures, from the town hall.

The opening of the summer parks and summer facilities for children, from the City Health and Recreation Department.

Educational television shows for the coming month, from the local TV stations.

5. Actual historical scenes or events in other countries can be dramatized to help children understand the event more fully. Often the entire class can take part in such dramatizations, no audience need watch because the emphasis is on participation and involvement to develop creativity and empathy. One group dramatized a Mexican Christmas, a pinata party and a Mexican fiesta. Every child played a role in keeping with the situation. Another group dramatized a medieval fair. Other events which lend themselves to total group dramatization are: a medieval tournament, a visit to a Spanish market place, the election of a president, a day in Plymouth, a trip to New York, an evening around a campfire, the meeting of an Indian council, a visit to a carnival, and a day at Fort Niagara.

6. In the game "Who Am I?" one child sits before a group and tells about himself, stopping once in awhile to act out certain parts of his life. The rest of the class is to guess who he is. In Mr. Jones's class, one boy acted as Ben Franklin and told about his boyhood. He dramatized his experimentation with a kite to discover electricity and his invention of the Franklin stove. This particular dramatization was

FIGURE 7–2. *The book opens . . .*

so well done that Mr. Jones used it as a means of introducing "Ben and Me" to the class.

7. Individual dramatic interpretation can be encouraged with a "You Are There" game. Children dramatize an historical even and the rest of the class tells what it is. The Boston Tea Party, the assassination of Lincoln, the launching of a space ship, and innumerable other events lend themselves well to this sort of treatment.

8. Historical events can be dramatized in social studies to make history more realistic and to develop creativity. Many scenes lend

FIGURE 7–3. *Chapter II:* In a Chapel

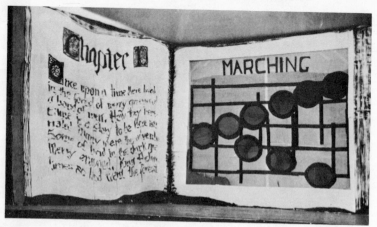

FIGURE 7–4. *Chapter III:* A Marching Song. Heads for notes and each sings his own song.

themselves well to such dramatic interpretation: the landing of the Pilgrims, the signing of the Declaration of Independence, a meeting of the United Nations Security Council, the inauguration of the president, the daily life of a cowboy, a day in a colonial school and many others.

9. The format of a popular radio program of a few years back, "Minute Dramas," lends itself well to creative development. First an opening scene is described and then the children make up and dramatize an ending with no preparation. For example: "You are at

FIGURE 7–5. *Chapter IV:* King Richard's Banquet Hall

the airport waiting for a plane and suddenly a strange man rushes up to you, clasps your hand, calls you by name and says, 'I haven't seen you for years. It's just luck that I should see you now! I am in deep trouble and I need your help!' "

10. Various forms of dramatization lend themselves well to creative book reports (See Book II, *Creative Teaching of the Language Arts in the Elementary School,* Chapter V and Book III, *Creative Teaching of Reading and Literature in the Elementary School,* Chapter VI) for some illustrations of this type of activity.

11. Place five unrelated objects in a bag such as a thumb tack, a water pistol, a hair curler, a stick of gum and a measuring cup. Divide the class into groups of five. Each group takes a bag and must construct a story using all of the five objects which they then dramatize for the rest of the class. Children enjoy making up the bags for each other.

12. In fractured dramas, instead of dramatizing stories exactly as they are written, children are encouraged to change the endings. Thus in "Casey at the Bat," Casey does *not* strike out. Comic relief is encouraged and children have a way to expend the wisecracks, which they so enjoy at this age, in a legitimate and acceptable manner. A modern parody on "Little Red Riding Hood," by one sixth grade, had Red Riding Hood playing the part of a communist spy and the wolf as a symbol for Russia. The entire production was hilarious and creative.

One sixth grade group performed a fractured interpretation of *Romeo and Juliet.* The entire balcony scene was played with Romeo using television commercials in wooing Juliet, such as "Thine eyes glow like coals, my love. Does thou use Maybelline? And thy lips— truly a product of Helena Rubenstein with the smile of Gleam so easy to come by."

Children are jolted into breaking away from traditional patterns of thinking in developing new ideas or inventing new endings. The imaginative aspects of their thinking are brought into play. Creative ideation, through the use of modification, minification, elaboration, substitution and other techniques mentioned in Chapter I, is brought into play.

It is important to realize that taking liberties with established pieces of literature should not detract from the literature itself. It can add meaning and beauty to it if the children are able to catch the feeling of the author's writing or show his skill by use of contrasts. The ability to form analogies is a part of creative thinking. Constant use of symbolism, as in the incident where Red Riding Hood was a Russian Spy, is a rich experience in creative thinking for children. Empathy is developed, analogies are created, subtleties are imagined and symbolism takes on real meaning. Each of these skills is a strong force in developing creative thinking.

13. Children enjoy dramatizing scenes from their favorite stories, movies and television shows.

Summary

Dramatics, in one form or another, constitute a normal creative outlet for human beings in all stages of their development. It is often man's basic system of communication. To deny its development is to deny his full creative growth and his full communicative ability. Dramatics should legitimately play an important role in the elementary school program every day.

TO THE COLLEGE STUDENT

1. Observe the director of your college drama department. Is he a creative director? How can a director be creative in attempting to produce a play which is already written? Is it possible to develop creativity in college students through the production of classical plays?

2. Try writing a short play in class, perhaps using music in it. What skills are needed to be able to write a play? Do you have them? Did you follow any of the steps in the creative act as mentioned in Chapter I when you wrote your play? What opportunities for creative development does the presentation of the play afford? Pinpoint the time in the total act of play producing when creativity may be nurtured.

3. Observe carefully, and draw the attention of your college classmates to, really outstanding creative products of current interest in your environment. Note especially creative television shows, cartoons, musicals, dramas, musical compositions, types of architecture, editorials, short stories, paintings, etc. Keep the bulletin board in your classroom full of examples of creative work.

4. Drama can be very subtle and can put across political and sociological issues better than any other means. Read Arthur Miller's, "The Crucible."

5. Make a list of other plays in which the creativity of the author brings home a message with dramatic impact.

TO THE CLASSROOM TEACHER

1. List all the ways you can think of to include some form of dramatics in your school program in the coming weeks. Observe your children carefully when they are engaged in play-acting. Sometimes this is the best way to learn things about your children which you did not know.

2. Instead of using real life situations, ask your children to dramatize abstractions such as, "Show me fear," "Show me orange," "Show me fever."

3. What is the value of presenting a play at the P.T.A. which has been written by the teacher, produced by the teacher and where the children repeat memorized lines?

4. How well did Mr. Randall set conditions for creative development in the story at the beginning of this chapter? Which of the psychological conditions mentioned in Chapter V did he consider? Which socio-emotional factors? Intellectual?

TO THE COLLEGE STUDENT AND
THE CLASSROOM TEACHER

1. Puppets often provide a projective technique for children. Why will some children shy away from actual play-acting before a group, but enter fully into dramatics through the use of puppets?

2. Think of all the projective techniques you can use in a classroom which will help children gain emotional release through the use of dramatics.

3. Reread the quotations at the beginning of each chapter in this book and note the person who made each. Would you say that

people in all walks of life are concerned about the development of this precious commodity? Broaden this concept by rereading the quotes at the beginning of each chapter in the other books of this series.

4. Ask children to dramatize inanimate objects and see what they can do. Objects you might suggest are a paper clip, a thumb tack, a fountain pen, a bed spring or a pair of scissors.

5. Ask some children to dramatize noises such as the wail of a siren, the scratch of chalk on the chalkboard, the sound of a flow pen squeaking, a lawn mower or a snowflake. Ask some adults to do this first, then ask the children. Which group is more original, more creative and less inhibited? Explain the differences you observe.

6. Design a playground that is ideally equipped to encourage dramatic play.

7. Observe the adults around you. Can you detect any of them playing a role to gain status and attention? For instance, can you find in your group of acquaintances the movie queen, the poor little rich girl, the typical football hero, the bookworm, the nonconformist, the leader, the politician or the apple polisher?

8. Write short descriptions of the typical role of the college professor (i.e., absent-minded, tweed-jacketed, pipe-smoking), the brain, the vampire, the wolf. How well do these stereotypes compare with the people you have labeled as such?

SELECTED BIBLIOGRAPHY

ANDREWS, GLADYS. *Creative Rhythmic Movement for Children.* Englewood Cliffs: Prentice-Hall, Inc., 1954.

ANDREWS, GLADYS. JEANNETTE SAURBORN and ELSA SCHNEIDER, *Physical Education for Today's Boys and Girls.* Boston: Allyn and Bacon, Inc., 1960.

BURGER, ISABEL. *Creative Play Activity.* New York: A. S. Barnes & Co., 1950.

HARTLEY, RUTH E., LAWRENCE K. FRANK, and ROBERT M. GOLDENSON, *Understanding Children's Play.* New York: Columbia University Press, 1952.

ILG, FRANCES, LOUISE B. AMES, EVELYN W. GOODENOUGH and IRENE B. ANDERSON, *The Gesell Institute Party Book.* New York: Harper & Row, Publishers, Inc., 1956.

Lease, Ruth and Geraldine B. Siks, *Creative Dramatics in Home, School and Community*. New York: Harper & Row, Publishers, Inc. 1952.

Siks, Geraldine Brain, *Creative Dramatics: An Art for Children*. New York: Harper & Row, 1958.

Williams, Helen V., *Puppets Go to School*. Philadelphia: Winston Company, 1955.

Conclusion: The Creative Teacher

Creativity in teaching can thus be judged by the quality of opportunities actually provided by a teacher for young people to have educative experiences.[1]

ALICE MIEL

Introduction

The first real day of spring had arrived! The children knew it because the sun was shining and there was a new feel to the air! It smelled like spring! It looked like spring! It tasted like spring! It felt like spring! And, just to remove any doubts, here came Lanny into the fifth grade room clutching the first bouquet of daffodils!

After the long, hard winter their fragile brightness was captured sunlight. The children exclaimed over the beauty of the flowers. Miss Orr, too, was enthusiastic over their appearance. At once the problem arose as to what was to be done with them. Where should they be put so all might enjoy them?

The children gathered in a semi-circle at the front of the room for their planning period and the first problem of the day was to determine what should be done with Lanny's flowers.

Mickey suggested they be placed in the front of the room where they could be seen by everyone all day. An extra desk was pushed up front and two boys moved it around until the most appropriate place was found. Then Lanny chose a vase for the flowers from the supply cupboard in the back of the room. She selected a low, flat vase because, she said, "The leaves are pretty too, and they will show up better in a vase like this."

. The vase was placed on the table and the flowers were put in a needle holder. Janet said, "I don't think the flowers show up too well—there is too much on the wall behind them."

---

[1] Alice Miel, *Creative Teaching: Invitations and Instances.* (Belmont: Wadsworth Publishing Company, Inc., 1961), p. 9.

"Let's put a screen behind the desk to shut off the wall," added Nanine.

Some boys rolled up a burlap-covered screen which was used often for moveable bulletin board exhibits and placed it behind the flowers. The group agreed that this was much better.

"Now, I don't think the flowers show up well enough," said Dorothy. "Each one is so pretty, yet all I see is a big yellow spot."

Miss Orr suggested that it would be an addition if each flower's individual shape could be seen.

"We could cut the stems different lengths," said Andy, "and that will help each flower to show."

No sooner said than done. Lanny rearranged the flowers so they were on various eye levels—each blossom an individual form.

"I would like it better if we had a colored background," Emily evaluated. "The tan burlap is sorta dead. Daffodils make me think of *live* things and spring."

Two of the boys brought up remnants of colored cloth from the supply cupboard. Different colors were held up until a plain, light green was agreed upon. This was pinned over the burlap screen and carried down and draped over the desk, forming a background and a base for the flowers. The effect was lovely, but the children were not yet satisfied. One of the boys had seen two little yellow china ducks in the closet when he secured the cloth. "I think these would look nice in the arrangement," he said. "Ducks come in the spring too. Besides, if we put the ducks in the picture it will carry the yellow to another part of the arrangement." He tried the ducks at the base of the vase, facing them away from the flowers.

Immediately Janet commented, "Turn the ducks around, Dick; with their backs to the flowers your eyes go in two directions. If they face the flowers, then your eyes are drawn in toward the flowers and the flowers are the most important part of the picture."

The ducks were turned around; the group agreed that the effect was better.

"I'd like a frame for our arrangement," said Dale. "Let's try the picture frame that is in the cupboard." He found the frame, which had been painted white for another purpose, and held it in front of the arrangement. The group agreed the frame tied the picture together but that the white was too stark; it detracted from the flowers. So Dale nailed the frame on a wooden block so it would stand alone and two of the girls dabbed a gray tempera paint on it to soften the color. While this was going on, the class went on with its planning for the day. When the frame was finished and placed before the arrangement, the class evaluated the arrangement. It was lovely, but Bruce was still not satisfied. "It needs height," he said. "There is too much at the bottom of the picture and nothing at the top." Lanny added, "There isn't any gray in the picture either—only in the frame and I think we should have some gray somewhere in the arrangement."

Someone finally suggested a dead twig might do the trick so Bruce took off to the orchard behind the school to find one. He returned with a gnarled piece of apple tree branch and set it in a wad of clay behind the daffodils. The children responded with exclamations of delight at the effect. All agreed that the arrangement was complete—it was beautiful.

It was not only beautiful but symbolic. The dead twig denoted the passing of winter, the fresh green of spring was represented in the tapestry and leaves of the flowers, the return of the sun appeared in the daffodils, and the resurrection of life in the baby ducklings. All day long the children enjoyed their creation. All day long they brought visitors in to see their arrangement.

Mary said, "We really painted a picture today with materials instead of paints. I'd like to call it 'Still Life.'" So the picture was called "Still Life" by the fifth grade class.

Still life in the arrangement, but not still life in that fifth grade room. It was an active, creative room, with a creative teacher. Creative things happened there. They happened because Miss Orr believed they should happen and she set conditions for them to happen.

There are reasons why Miss Orr believes experiences like this should take place in her classroom. She feels that the creative development of the children in her classroom is one of her most important objectives.

Experiences such as this are some of the truest and most lifelike ways through which she can develop creativity in children. This wise teacher capitalized on a real experience which had been unplanned. The groundwork she had laid was not unplanned, however, as was evidenced by the manner in which this class handled the situation. A consciousness of beauty and emphasis on a beautiful, livable environment had been an aim of this teacher ever since the children came to school in the fall. Her room had been set up to receive them. Centers of interests were full of interesting and enriching materials. The room itself was attractive and home-like. Materials to promote free expression were abundant. And the teacher, herself, had planned many enriching experiences to build up the creative abilities in her children. The story of the daffodils was simply an evaluation of the results of her good work. These children could create on their own. They were conscious of relatedness of materials. They were sensitive to texture, color and harmony. Their still life showed a consciousness of design through line, form, color and light. They were thoughtful of organization and plan; they could see and understand relationships. They were acquainted with divergent thinking, with problem-solving and with open-ended experiences in many media. These children were developing their creative abilities.

And it had happened because Miss Orr had *set conditions for it to happen*.

There are differences between the creative and the uncreative teacher. Bond attempted to discover those traits which make superior teachers and he concluded that creativeness is essential as a contributor to superior teaching success and that it is proportionally lacking with teachers of inferior ability.

A test of thirty-two measured traits disclosed significant differences between the creative and less creative teachers. Chief among these traits were *resourcefulness* and *initiative*.[2]

There are blocks that stand in the way of creative teaching. Biber contends that individuality among children has been lost under the impact of socializing pressures in child rearing and the realities of teaching children in a classroom. She feels that education has imposed a structure of didactic instruction, right-wrong criteria, dominance of the logical-objective over the intuitive-subjective on the learning child so early in his life that his creative potential is often inhibited. The learning of skills, facts and tools is important but the problem lies in how skillfully a teacher can place these offerings within the developmental sequence that stretches between the phase of the exposure and that of mastery and how well conditions may be set to develop creativity between these phases. She suggests that creative teaching means allowing the child freedom to incubate and providing experiences to be incubated, to help sustain a mood of searching, to tolerate a degree of chaos and irrelevance and freedom from social regimentation, and finally, to represent the evaluative judgment of the adult world. Creative teaching takes responsibility

2 J. A. Bond, "Analysis of Observed Traits of Teachers Rated Superior in Demonstrating Creativeness in Teaching," in *Journal of Educational Research*, LIII (1959) pp. 8–12.

for stimulating, guiding, channeling, presenting and explaining. It cannot be accomplished by a passive teacher.[3]

Torrance has listed six blocks to creativity:

1. Premature attempts to eliminate fantasy; 2. Placing too many restrictions on the child's desire to manipulate and on his curiosity; 3. Overemphasis on the sex role—limiting the activities of boys to socially accepted "boy" acts and girls to "girl" acts; 4. Overemphasis on prevention from trying things; 5. Induction of fear and timidity as a means of control; 6. Overemphasis on verbal skills.[4]

Certainly these findings have tremendous implications for the classroom teacher.

Creative teachers differ from uncreative teachers in other ways also. The one sees education as that agency by which knowledge is perpetuated while the other sees education as that process by which happy, contributing human beings are produced. Miss Orr is one of the latter, as are the many other teachers whose classrooms have been described in these pages. So are all teachers who see their job as one of setting conditions so creativity can emerge and meaningful learning can take place.

So are *you!* You are the creative teacher. You may not think so. You may say in all sincerity, "I cannot draw or paint," or "I don't know where people get ideas like the ones in this book—I never have them." You will feel inferior or insecure in believing this and will dismiss creative teaching from your conscience as something that belongs to a talented few.

But, wait a minute. A teacher can be creative if she can't draw a straight line. She can be creative if she never has a smash-bang idea. That is so because *she can still draw out the creative powers of the children even if her own creative powers have been suppressed.*

That is what we have been saying in this book. To be a creative teacher requires understanding more than talent, feelings and empathy more than knowledge, a setting of conditions more than some unique teaching skills. Let's look again at that which makes creative teaching:

1. Creative teaching is that teaching which is dedicated to the development of the uniqueness of every child.

[3] Barbara Biber, "Premature Structuring as a Deterrent to Creativity," *American Journal of Orthopsychiatry*, XXIX (1959) pp. 280–90.

[4] E. P. Torrance, "Current Research on the Nature of Creative Talent," in *Journal of Counseling Psychology*, VI, No. 4 (1959) pp. 309–16.

2. Because uniqueness is not brought forth in a sterile, unchallenging situation, creative teaching means that conditions must be set in each classroom to provide for the child's physical comfort, to challenge his intellect to the utmost, to provide the proper, positive, emotional tension and a comfortable social atmosphere.

3. The process of creating involves decision-making, passing judgment, choosing, selecting, perceiving, analyzing, divergent thinking, uncommonness of response, flexibility and fluency of ideas. The creative teacher teaches by problem-solving techniques in all areas so that children are in situations where these traits are constantly being developed.

4. The creative teacher helps children to identify problems and clarify them, and then she must set them free to create a solution. Creativity in itself cannot be taught; we can only set conditions for it to appear.

5. Under indoctrinary teaching, children's products all look alike. The creative teacher, however, never will look for differences in responses rather than likenesses as a measure of her ability to develop the uniqueness in each individual.

6. The creative teacher will realize that the child's work reveals his outlook and his feelings about the world around him. She will, therefore accept and respect his creative efforts even though they may seem immature.

7. She will recognize various stages of creative development and will not expect the immature child to create in any new media at a top level of performance or according to adult standards.

8. The creative teacher will not expect children to be artists, poets, composers, politicians or architects, because they are not. They are children and as children they think and feel their own way. They are like artists and poets because creativity is an inborn trait and in expressing it they use the tools of the artist or the poet, but they are not as mature, they do not have as much experience or as many concepts as the mature creator, nor have they mastered his skills.

9. The creative teacher understands that the creative process leads children to independence: independent thinking, independent choices, independent ability to solve problems and independent human relationships. Creative teaching gives the child self-confidence, a faith in himself and ultimate self-realization.

10. The creative teacher guides the child in all forms of self-expression, adds richness in creative exploration to all his experiences in the schoolroom, stimulates his thinking, provokes his curiosity and recognizes him for his own values and competencies and not those of others.

11. The creative teacher removes excessive competition from her classroom and replaces it with a spirit of cooperation and effective human relationships.

12. The creative teacher will evaluate the effectiveness of her teaching by the behavior of the children as much as by the products of these children. She will note the degree to which her pupils are gaining self-confidence. She will note the degree to which they are sensitive to their

own possibilities and realistic about their own capabilities. She will study their behavior in terms of their awareness of their own environment, their ability to react to it and their eagerness to make unique contributions to their school, home, neighborhood and the world.

13. Creative teaching is not a supplement to teaching nor is it an adornment to practices. It is a method of teaching by itself. A new approach, a new outlook on the purpose of education. Much of what currently constitutes present-day teaching practices is good and should be retained, but current methodology needs to be evaluated so that those practices which keep children from developing their creative power can be discarded.

There are hundreds of creative teachers already at work. They are creative because their whole philosophy is centered around the self-actualization of each child so that he may fulfill his potential in life. These teachers care about individuals and realize the importance of salvaging all the creative potential in our democratic society.

Each of the above understandings is within the realm of comprehension of any teacher. No talent is necessary for these understandings. Too much talent may be just as much an obstacle in the attainment of these understandings as none at all. It is how talent is used that counts, and it can be harmful when not used in accordance with the above basic principles. Actually, all teachers have those qualities and skills needed to perform at the creative level: a knowledge of subject matter, a knowledge of children, an understanding of the creative process, a set of skills in using material and in dealing with children.

If teachers brand themselves as uncreative, it is probably due to two things: first, they do not really understand what creativity is or how to develop it. We hope this book has helped to develop that understanding.

Second, they may feel uncreative because they work in an environment where conditions have not been set for them to release their own potential creative power. Just as teachers must set conditions in the classroom for children to create, so must administrators set conditions in the school so the teachers may be creative. The dominated, pressured teacher who has all her duties spelled out, who is restricted to limited amounts of freedom, who does not take part in setting school policy and practice, and who is not involved in solving school problems or developing her own professional learnings is not likely to be free enough to be herself in her own classroom. The negative tension which motivates her may keep her from being an individual who functions as a creative power in her classroom; she becomes a puppet who unfortunately often releases her own tensions on the children. Creative teachers will emerge when top priority in our merit ratings is placed on creativeness and when administrators take it upon themselves to set conditions to free teachers by encouraging individuality among them, and doing all in their power to facilitate teaching. Both administrators and teachers must work hand in hand toward creative development. Administration can be as creative as teaching.

Laura Zirbes, in her book, "Spurs to Creative Teaching," gives ideas of the differences in creative individuals and uncreative ones. She pairs the contrasting characteristics of creative growth and the educational status quo as follows:

from stereotyped conformity *toward* free expression
from passive compliance *toward* active identification
from imposed direction *toward* cooperative planning
from coercive requirements *toward* voluntary commitments
from mass handling *toward* individual guidance
from extrinsic motivation *toward* intrinsic value concerns
from submissive acquiescence *toward* wholehearted involvement
from restrictive domination *toward* responsible self-direction
from stultifying repression *toward* spontaneity
from the fixing of habits and skills *toward* the cultivation of flexible adaptive responses to life-related situations.[5]

It would seem that every teacher and every administrator in the profession today should use this list as a goal for his own performance in the classroom. With the realization that only she has the power to make his teaching and administrating creative, he can set about to revitalize his own teaching and supervision by rededicating himself.

Young people entering the profession must pursue creative ways of learning by maintaining their dedication and enthusiasm for teaching and using this check list as an unwavering goal for which to strive in the exciting, adventurous years of teaching which lie ahead.

TO ALL READERS

Some tapes by Laura Zirbes are available on this topic. The following are recommended for class listening and discussion:

[5] Laura Zirbes, *Spurs to Creative Teaching*. (New York: G. P. Putnam's Sons, 1959), p. xiii.

No Z- 7 What Creative Teaching Means, 19 min.
No Z-15 The Emotional Climate of Schools, 13 min.
No Z-27 Creative Thinking and Creative Teaching for Creative Living, Two parts, 55 min.

SELECTED BIBLIOGRAPHY

ALEXANDER, WILLIAM M. *Are You a Good Teacher?* New York: Holt, Rinehart and Winston, Inc., 1959.

ASHTON-WARNER, SYLVIA. *Spinster.* New York: Simon and Schuster, Inc., 1959.

BEAUCHAMP, GEORGE A. *Basic Dimensions of Elementary Method.* Boston: Allyn and Bacon, Inc., 1959.

BYERS, LORETTA and ELIZABETH IRISH. *Success in Student Teaching.* Boston: D. C. Heath and Co., 1961.

CRAWFORD, ROBERT P. *The Techniques of Creative Thinking.* New York: Hawthorn Books, Inc., 1954.

Department of Classroom Teachers, *Conditions of Work for Quality Teaching.* Washington, D.C.: National Education Association, 1959.

GHISELIN, BREWSTER. *The Creative Process.* New York: Mentor Press, 1955.

HARRISON, RAYMOND H. and LAWRENCE E. GOWIN. *The Elementary Teacher in Action.* San Francisco: Wadsworth Publishing Co., Inc., 1958.

LOGAN, LILLIAN and VIRGIL G. LOGAN. *Teaching the Elementary School Child.* Boston: Houghton Mifflin Co., 1961.

MACKINNAN, DONALD W. "What Makes a Person Creative?" *Saturday Review* (February 10, 1962), pp. 5–7.

MIEL, ALICE (ed.). *Creativity in Teaching: Invitations and Instances.* Belmont, California: Wadsworth Publishing Company, Inc., 1961.

MOUSTAKAS, CLARK, *The Self.* New York: Harper & Row, Publishers, Inc., 1956.

MURPHY, GARDNER. *Human Potentialities.* New York: Basic Books, Inc., 1958.

OSBORN, ALEX F. *Applied Imagination,* rev. ed. New York: Charles Scribner's Sons, 1957.

PATRICK, CATHERINE. *What Is Creative Thinking?* New York: Philosophical Library, Inc., 1955.

VANDER WERF, LESTER S. *How To Evaluate Teachers and Teaching.* New York: Holt, Rinehart and Winston, Inc., 1958.

ZIRBES, LAURA. *Encouraging Creativity in Student Teaching.* Cedar Falls: Association for Student Teaching, 1956.

Index

Activities:
  for dramatics in primary grades, 157–159
  for dramatic play in intermediate grades, 159–170
  for intermediate grade music, 113–125
  for primary music, 111–113
  in rhythm and dance in intermediate grades, 144–146
  in rhythm and dance, primary grades, 139–144
  to stimulate creative thinking through art, 73–74
Aesthetics; values in music, 103–104
Aesthetic sense, development of, 36
Andrews, Gladys:
  cited, 137
  quoted, 129
Andrews, Michael, quoted 17, 167
Appreciation, activities in art, 73–74
Art:
  aesthetic sense and, 36
  classics and, 37
  communication and, 19–23
  conditions for development, 24–25
  conditions for teaching, 19–39
  creative abilities and, 38–39
  creative teaching in, 17–44, 67–90
  definition, 17
  as developmental, 23–24
  experience and application, 43–44
  goals, 18
  individuality and, 18–19
  nature of, 18–44
  poster making, 35–36
  processes and, 19–23
  role of specialist, 39–42
  stages of growth, 20–25
  stimuli for, 25–36
  teaching example, 25–26
  unit teaching and, 28–30
Art expression, experiences to develop, 69–90
Art teaching, ideas, 89–90
Axline, Virginia, cited, 60

Barkan, Manuel, quoted, 3
Biber, Barbara, cited, 178
Blotter-printing, 78
Bond, J. A., cited, 177

Calypso, 120
Candle-making, 80–81
Child development:
  art and, 23–24
  art in intermediate grades, 32–34
Christmas tree ornaments, 76
Classics, in art, 37
Communication, art and, 19–23
Composers, stories about, 122–123
Conditions:
  for creative teaching, 9
  for art development, 24–25
  for dramatic play in intermediate grades, 161–170
  for dramatization in primary grades, 155–159
  for primary grade music activities, 105–113
  for teaching art, 19–39
Conformity, creativity and, 6
Construction, 81

Corrugated cardboard designs, 76
Crayon, melted, 89
Creative arts, nature of, 3–63
Creative ideation, as method, 12
Creative teacher, 174–181
Creative teaching:
  of art, 67–90
  art example, 25–26
  basic principles, 7–12
  conditions for, 9
  criteria for, 178–180
  democratic processes and, 11
  dramatization and, 150–170
  evaluation and, 11
  example in art, 25–26
  fourth grade illustration of dra-
    matics, 150–154
  illustration, creative arts, 174–
    181
  kindergarten music illustration,
    99–102
  knowledges and, 10
  music and, 94–125
  preconscious thinking and, 8
  success and, 10
  through rhythms and dance,
    129–147
Creative thinking, experiences in
  art, 73–90
Creative writing, music and, 117–
  125
Creativity:
  conformity and, 6
  definition, 4
  development through rhythms
    and dance in intermediate
    grades, 144–146
  development through rhythms
    and dance in primary grades,
    139–144
  intelligence and, 4–5
  music as contribution to develop-
    ment, 104–105
  nature through art, 67–90
  originality and, 7
  outcomes and, 8
  principles, 3–13
  as process and product, 5
  research in, 3–12

  through intermediate grade music
    activities, 113–125
  through primary grade music
    activities, 105–113
  unconscious mind and, 6

Dance:
  conditions for development, 130–
    136
  creative teaching of, 129–147
  definition, 129
  movement and, 137–138
  nature of teaching, 53–54
  rhythms and, 53–54
  teacher's role, 136–138
Deferred judgment, as unique
  method, 12
Democratic processes, creative
  teaching and, 11
Dramatic play, 56–58, 155–157
  intermediate grades, 170
Dramatics:
  creative, 55–60
  dramatic play, 56–58
  fourth grade illustration, 150–
    154
  free play, 58
  nature of teaching, 55–60
  play therapy and, 59–60
  primary grade conditions, 155–
    159
  role-playing and, 58–59
  structured, 60
Dramatization:
  creative teaching and, 150–170
  primary grade conditions, 155–
    159
  structured, 60

Egg carton art, 89
Ellsworth, Maud, quoted, 17, 67
Emotional conditions for teaching
  music, 99–103
Evaluation, creative teaching and,
  11
Experience:
  aesthetic values in music, 103–
    104

Experience (*Cont.*)
  application in art, 43–44
  in art units, 28–30
  creative thinking in art, 73–90
  to develop art expression, inter-
    mediate grades, 70–82
  to develop art expression, pri-
    mary grades, 69–70
  in music, 98–99

Film, making, 73–74
Flannel board:
  art abstracts and, 76
  paintings, 89
Fleming, Robert, cited, 137
Flower arrangements, 85
Forms, variation in, 75
Frank, Laurence K., cited, 58
Free play, 58
Frosting, 86
Fun songs, 117–118

Glass art, 81–82
Goldensen, Robert, cited, 58
Greeting card art, 86
Growth, stages in art development,
  20–25

Hartley, Ruth E., cited, 58

Individuality, art and, 18–19
Inner tube prints, 80
Instruments:
  construction of, 109–110
  music and, 108
  songs about, 119
  stories about, 121–122
  use of, 110
Intellectual conditions, for creative
  teaching, 9–10
Intelligence, creativity and, 4–5
Intermediate grades:
  developing creativity through
    rhythms and dance, 144–146
  dramatic play, 159–170
  experiences for art expression,
    70–72
  music activities, 113–125

Keltman, Gunild, cited, 114
Kindergarten, illustration for music,
  99–102
Knowledges, creative teaching and,
  10

Limericks, 123
Lowenfeld, Viktor, cited, 23

Mask-making, 87
Mead, Margaret, quoted, 94
Methods, unique for creative teaching, 11–12
Miel, Alice, quoted, 174
Mobiles, cut paper, 74
Modeling, 87
Movement, dance and, 137–138
Music:
  activities for teaching, 111–125
  appreciation, 123–125
  calypso, 120
  composer stories, 122–123
  conditions for teaching, 95–105
  creative teaching and, 94–125
  creative writing and, 117–125
  creativity and, 104–105
  exploration, 108
  fun songs, intermediate grades,
    117–118
  instruments and, 107, 108, 119–
    122
  intermediate grade illustrations,
    113–125
  listening, 107
  making instruments, 109–110
  moving to, 107
  nature of, 49–53
  nature of teaching, 49–53
  objectives in elementary school,
    50, 94
  role singing in primary grades,
    107
  subject matter for, 97
  unit teaching and, 98–99

Open-ended stories, for dramatic
  play, 163–165
Orff, Carl, cited, 114
Originality, creativity and, 7

Osborn, Alex F., cited, 11
Outcomes, creativity and, 8
Overview, 66

Painting, words, 84
Parnes, Sidney J., cited, 11
Physical conditions, for creative teaching, 9
Plaster of Paris, 86–87
Plato, quoted, 49
Play therapy, 59–60
Pomeroy, Sally, cited, 114
Posters, example as art form, 35–36
Preconscious, as a principle, 8
Primary grades:
    developing creativity through rhythms and dance, 139–144
    experiences for art expression, 69–70
    music activities, 105–113
Principles:
    of creative teaching, 7–12
    of creativity, 3–13
Printing processes, 77–78
Processes, art and, 19–23
Psychological conditions, for creative teaching, 9
Puppetry, in art, 87–88

Readiness, in music, 52
Recordings, intermediate grades, 113
Resist process, 82
Rhythms:
    creative teaching of, 129–147
    dance and, 53–54
Rogers, Carl, quoted, 17
Role-playing, dramatics and, 58–59

Sand moulding, 84–85
Saurborn, Jeanette, cited, 137
Schneider, Elsa, cited, 137

Scratch drawings, 85
Sculpting, 85
Self-portraits, 88–89
Shakespeare, quoted, 150
Skills, of evaluation, 244–264
Slides, making, 84
Smith, James A., cited, 6, 28, 58, 59, 60, 74, 103, 112, 114
Socio-emotional conditions, for creative teaching, 10
Space relationships, 76
Specialists, role in art teaching, 39–42
Spinning tops, as art project, 75–76
Stabiles, in art, 75
Stages, in developmental art, 23–24
Staple designs, 86
Stimuli:
    for art experiences, 25–36
    for musical experiences, 97–99
String balloons, 82–84
String designs, 82
String painting, 84
Stuffed animals, 77
Success, creative teaching and, 10

Teacher, role in teaching dance, 136–138
Tensions, creativity and, 7
Tin can art, 85–86
Tin foil craft, 77
Torrance, E. P., cited, 178
Trips, for sketching, 74

Unconscious, creativity and the, 6
Unit teaching:
    art experiences and, 28–30
    experiences in music, 98–99

Whipped soap art, 87

Zirbes, Laura, quoted, 181